DULUTH

DULUTH

An Urban Biography

TONY DIERCKINS

MINNESOTA
HISTORICAL
SOCIETY PRESS

CLEAN
WATER
LAND &
LEGACY
AMENDMENT

Cities, like people, are always changing, and the history of that change
is the city's biography. The Urban Biography Series illuminates the unique character
of each city, weaving in the hidden stories of place, politics, and identity that
continue to shape its residents' lives.

mnhspress.org

The Minnesota Historical Society Press is a member of the Association of University Presses.

Manufactured in the United States of America

10 9 8 7 6 5 4 3 2 1

♾ The paper used in this publication meets the minimum requirements
of the American National Standard for Information Sciences—Permanence for
Printed Library Materials, ANSI Z39.48–1984.

International Standard Book Number
ISBN: 978-1-68134-159-0 (paper)
ISBN: 978-1-68134-160-6 (e-book)

Library of Congress Cataloging-in-Publication Data

Names: Dierckins, Tony, author.
Title: Duluth : an urban biography / Tony Dierckins.
Description: Saint Paul : Minnesota Historical Society Press, 2020. |
Includes bibliographical references and index. | Summary: "In this richly
textured urban biography, author Tony Dierckins highlights fascinating stories
of the city of Duluth, Minnesota: Its significance in the Ojibwe people's migration.
The failed copper rush along Lake Superior's North Shore that started the city's growth.
The natural port on the St. Louis River that made shipping its first and most important
business. The legend of the digging of the ship canal. The unique aerial
transfer bridge and its successor, the lift bridge. The city's remarkable park system.
The 1920 lynching of three African American circus workers. The Glensheen murders.
The evolution of the city's east-west divide. Throughout the years, the big lake and river
have sustained Duluth's economy, shaped its residents' recreation, and attracted the
tourists who marvel at the city's beauty and cultural life"—Provided by publisher.
Identifiers: LCCN 2019057545 | ISBN 9781681341590 (paperback) |
ISBN 9781681341606 (ebook)
Subjects: LCSH: Duluth (Minn.)—History.
Classification: LCC F614.D8 D535 2020 | DDC 977.6/771—dc23
LC record available at https://lccn.loc.gov/2019057545

This and other Minnesota Historical Society Press books are
available from popular e-book vendors.

For

MARYANNE C. NORTON

Contents

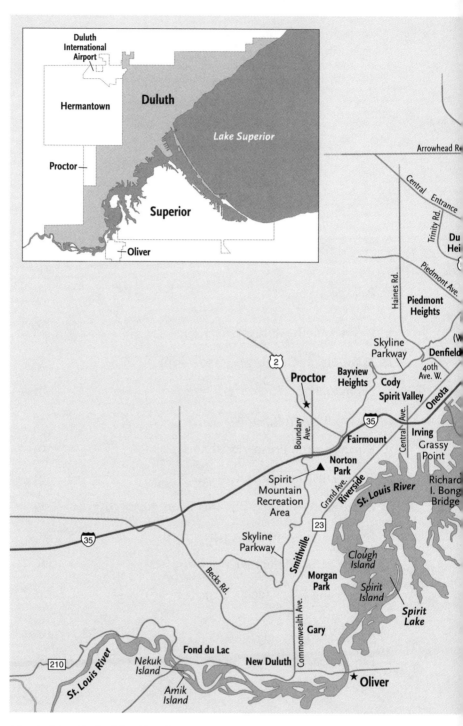

Map by Matt Kania, Map Hero Inc.

Prologue

Duluth, Minnesota, sits perched at the western tip of the Great Lakes, running twenty-eight miles along the northern shorelines of Lake Superior and its largest tributary, the St. Louis River—waterways that have profoundly shaped the city, not just geographically, but economically and culturally as well. By 1700 the natural harbor they formed provided a home for Ojibwe residents. In the mid-1800s, as the nation expanded westward, that harbor attracted those who saw its future as a great shipping center. The name "Duluth"—chosen to commemorate an ambitious and often arrogant seventeenth-century French soldier who once portaged over a sandbar separating the lake and river—first appeared on maps in 1856. Its strategic position and the surrounding region's abundant natural resources would help Duluth ride out dramatic economic ebbs and flows created by waves of panic, depression, and recession. Once a railroad arrived, wharves and docks blossomed along the bay, soon joined by warehouses, factories, and mills. Upstream, the river's rapids later turned turbines, producing the electricity that powered industry. Beyond acting as an anchorage for manufacturing and trade, the lake's and river's waters also provided food and offered endless recreational opportunities and natural beauty that have persistently drawn visitors to their shores. But those waters carried challenge and conflict as well, leaving little room to develop infrastructure, fueling a feud with Duluth's neighbor across the bay, and creating a geographic split that to this day divides the city economically and politically. And so the story of Duluth begins—and continues—where the lake and river converge.

CHAPTER 1

Before Duluth (To 1850)

The First Peoples

Lake Superior has drawn people to its western shores for millennia—long before anyone thought to name a community centered on its convergence with the St. Louis River "Duluth."

We can't know what the first peoples called themselves, but archaeologists—who name cultures and describe them by the artifacts they leave behind—refer to the people who first moved to the area about fourteen thousand years ago as Paleo-Indians. They hunted large game, including mastodons, at the end of the last Ice Age. About 7000 BCE, as the weather warmed, the large game died out, other foods became more plentiful, and the Eastern Archaic culture arose. People thrived along the developing Great Lakes, hunting a broad range of game with more effective tools, including some made of copper mined on Michigan's Keweenaw Peninsula and Isle Royale. Three thousand years ago, Woodland mound-building cultures followed; people grew corn, beans, and squash, made pottery, and established seasonal village sites.

By 1600, when European explorers began to write about the area, the people living in what is now northern Minnesota called themselves Dakota; their neighbors were the Assiniboine and Cree. The Dakota—the region's largest group, with a significant population on central Minnesota's Lake Mille Lacs—understand that they have always lived in what is now Minnesota. Dakota origin stories hold that the Dakota came

Formed by Fire and Ice

The forces that shaped Duluth's geography occurred during the planet's formation several billion years ago, in the Precambrian era. Basalt and granite found along Lake Superior's western shore indicate volcanic and seismic activity, and according to geologist John C. Green, the landscape once featured "great mountain ranges, perhaps rivaling the Alps, which have since been eroded to the nub." Sandstone and slate deposits along the lake's south shore and up the St. Louis River to Cloquet speak of a vast sea that once covered the region. More volcanic eruptions and earthquakes were followed by more erosion.

About 1.8 million years ago a giant plume of molten rock melted and spread as it neared the surface, creating cracks in the earth's crust that allowed magma to burst through in what Green describes as "huge fountains of intensely glowing lava spurting up from fissures that extended for miles across a barren plain" forming a "huge, pancake-like lava flow" that spread for 24 million years.

The result was the Midcontinent Rift System, a geologic feature portions of which have been mapped in a dozen US states, with southern Ontario at its apex and stretching as far south as Oklahoma and Mississippi. Lake Superior sits near the top. As volcanic activity subsided, the heavy basalt it produced sank at the basin's center, forming a shallow sea that over the eons filled with sediment carried by streams, eventually creating a hard basalt bowl filled with soft sandstone. The region then stabilized until about two million years ago, when it started getting cold and fire finally gave way to ice.

It took a while, but during the Pleistocene epoch—roughly 2.5 million to 11,500 years ago—glaciers eventually reached as far south as modern Kansas. Throughout several periods of glacial advances and retreats, the ice and harder rock trapped within the glaciers scoured out the sedimentary rock, leaving behind basins that would be later filled by rivers and streams created by melting glaciers. The last of these formations—the Laurentide Ice Sheet—left behind large, proglacial lakes that developed into today's Great Lakes. One, glacial Lake Duluth, essentially covered the western end of modern Lake Superior west of Michigan's Upper Peninsula and Isle Royale. Lake Duluth sat about five hundred feet higher than Lake Superior does today and covered a much larger area, but during the past ten thousand years the lake drained via the St. Croix River watershed, at one point dipping so low that its western shore sat near today's Silver Bay, fifty-five miles northeast of Duluth, before it rose to its current level. Most of Duluth's Skyline Parkway follows the shoreline of glacial Lake Duluth.

The eventual draining of another glacial lake, St. Louis, created the river for which it is named. The St. Louis begins roughly seventy-five miles north and east of Duluth at Seven Beaver Lake and flows roughly southwesterly to Floodwood, forty-six miles west of Duluth, before turning southeasterly, then eastward, then south to Cloquet and on to Carlton. There it turns east and begins a steep descent through a gorge, creating a series of rapids or dalles (French for "gutters") which drop dramatically as the river makes its way down to Duluth's Fond du Lac neighborhood. There its waters become navigable, turning north as they pass Gary and New Duluth and widen into an estuary that includes Spirit Lake and spreads east past Grassy Point to become St. Louis Bay before emptying into Lake Superior. Along the way the river covers 192 miles, dropping from 1,669 to 602 feet above sea level while creating a 3,648-square-mile watershed.

Together Lake Superior and the St. Louis, with help from the Nemadji River, have created a natural haven. Over the eons, silt carried by the St. Louis and Nemadji collided with sand stirred up by Superior's natural, clockwise rotation, eventually creating four distinct sandbars. Duluth's Rice's Point and Superior's Conner's Point once formed the very western shore of the lake, but have since been supplanted by Minnesota and Wisconsin Points, together the largest naturally formed baymouth bar on the planet. These four bars formed a large, natural, and protected harbor that would eventually make them an ideal place to build a city—or two.

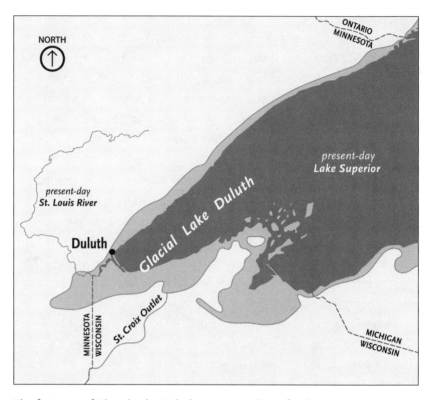

The footprint of Glacial Lake Duluth over an outline of today's Lake Superior and its largest tributary, the St. Louis River. *Map by Matt Kania, Map Hero Inc.*

from the stars. Most anthropologists believe that they are descended from the Woodland people.

The Ojibwe arrived in the seventeenth century following a long migration. In the 1840s, Ojibwe historian William Warren recorded an Ojibwe oral tradition that identifies the tribe's origins "on the shores of the Great Salt Water in the east," thought to be southeastern Ontario or New Brunswick. "While they were suffering the ravages of sickness and death," a prophecy told Ojibwe leaders to follow images of the megis shell, sacred to their Midewiwin beliefs, until they reached a place where "food grows on water"—a journey that lasted centuries. Competition for resources with other Native nations probably also played a part. By the 1500s, they were living at Bahweting at the mouth of the St. Marys River—today's Sault Ste. Marie—and trading with the French, who had laid claim to the Great Lakes region and beyond, calling it New France. Here the Ojibwe split into two groups, one moving north and west into what is now Canada and northeastern Minnesota, the other moving south and west into today's northern Michigan, Wisconsin, and eastern Minnesota.

From Sault Ste. Marie the southwestern Ojibwe pushed west to Moningwunakauning (Home of the golden-breasted woodpecker), known today as Madeline Island, largest of the Apostle Islands. In 1659 French Jesuit missionary Claude Allouez recorded that about four thousand Ojibwe lived in the Apostles and along the surrounding Chequamegon Bay. From this base on Lake Superior they ventured out to its western shores and indeed found food growing on water—manoomin (wild rice)—at Manidoo-zaaga'igan (Spirit Lake), a widening of the St. Louis River in what is now western Duluth. As the beaver population surrounding Chequamegon declined, the Ojibwe began resettling farther west along Lake Superior's south shore, the interior of today's Wisconsin and Minnesota, and up the St. Louis River to a point below its dalles. To the Ojibwe, Lake Superior was Gichigami (Great Sea) and the St. Louis River was Gichigami-ziibi (Great-Sea River). The Nemadji River, which helped form Wisconsin Point, they called Namanjii-ziibi (Left-Handed River) because it was located left of Gichigami-ziibi as one canoed from the lake through the natural entry between Minnesota and Wisconsin Points.

When the Ojibwe first arrived at Lake Superior, the Dakota had a presence on the western and southern shores of the lake, which they called Mdeyata. According to Ojibwe historian Anton Treuer, the Dakota welcomed the Ojibwe and the two peoples initially got along well as trading partners, creating an alliance in 1679 that lasted nearly sixty years. But following a conflict in 1736 that pitted the French, Cree, and Assiniboine against the Dakota, the Ojibwe were forced to choose which of their allies to side with, the Dakota or the French. Ultimately, they chose the French.

This led to a long and often violent conflict between the Dakota and Ojibwe over territory in Wisconsin and Minnesota. The Ojibwe eventually forced the Dakota west, and by 1770 they controlled the northern half of Minnesota. While the conflict continued, war parties became smaller, and by the 1850s both peoples faced a bigger concern: the massive influx of Americans and European immigrants. They fought no major battles after 1862, and in 1877 the Dakota gave the Ojibwe the ceremonial Big Drum as a peace offering, an action that ended the conflicts and resulted in peace between the tribes that continues today.

By 1800 the Ojibwe had established settlements on Minnesota and Wisconsin Points and along the St. Louis River nearly twenty miles upstream to Wayekwaagichigamiing (End of a great body of water) below the river's dalles. There they established a village centered on Nekuk (Otter) Island, tending vegetable gardens on the adjacent Amik (Beaver) Island and burying their dead in a cemetery located above the river's northern shore. Other burial sites were located on Minnesota, Wisconsin, Conner's, and Rice's Points. When maple sap flowed in the spring, sugarbush camps dotted the hillsides from Wayekwaagichigamiing to today's eastern Duluth. Spirit Lake, Spirit Island, Spirit Mountain, and Point of Rocks were considered sacred places. While it is unknown exactly when Wayekwaagichigamiing became an Ojibwe village, it was the site of the 1679 gathering that created the Dakota-Ojibwe alliance.

The Fur Trade

The first European to arrive at Lake Superior was Frenchman Etienne Brule in 1622, but he traveled no further than Isle Royale. The lake's western end and largest tributary weren't seen by non-Natives until Médard Chouart des Groseilliers and Pierre-Esprit Radisson showed up thirty-seven years later, reaching what is now Duluth in 1659.

The French had come to North America chiefly to find beaver fur and spread the gospel. From roughly 1550 to 1850, fashionable European gentlemen donned hats made primarily of beaver underfur. Consequently, by

1600 beavers had been hunted nearly to extinction in Western Europe, Scandinavia, and Russia. So France sent thousands of men to the New World, where the dam-building rodents were plentiful, to trade European goods for furs obtained by Native Americans. Catholic missionaries tagged along, hoping to convert the Native peoples to Christianity.

Brule, Groseilliers, and Radisson were fur traders. Claude Allouez established a mission at La Pointe (on Madeline Island) in 1665. Daniel Greysolon, Sieur du Lhut made it to Minnesota Point in 1679, carrying his canoe across the sandbar along a path near its base that the Ojibwe called Onigamiinsing (Little Portage). Described by friends (and himself) as an adventurous diplomat and by rivals as a scrupleless outlaw, du Lhut was seeking neither fur nor converts. He wanted to make a name for himself, either by discovering a water passage to the Pacific Ocean or by bringing the Ojibwe and Dakota together to ensure the Dakota would partner with the French in the fur trade—or both. While du Lhut never ventured further west than Lake Mille Lacs, he is traditionally credited for arranging the 1679 Dakota-Ojibwe gathering that began their fifty-seven-year alliance.

Du Lhut and his French contemporaries first called the great lake Lac Tracy, for the Marquis Alexandre Prouville de Tracy, governor of New France. Lac Tracy gave way to Lac Superior, which described the lake's position above or "superior to" Lake Huron, rather than its size. The French referred to the entire far-western portion of Lake Superior as Fond du Lac (Bottom of the Lake) and to the Ojibwe as Chippewa, based on a mispronunciation. (Ojibwe today are also considered Anishinaabe.) Early maps labeled the great river at the lake's western end Rivière du Fond du Lac, but by 1775 they called it St. Louis, likely for the French monarch and Catholic saint Louis IX.

Competition between France and England over fur and just about everything else in North America led to the French and Indian War, which began in 1754 and ended in a British victory with the 1763 Treaty of Paris. After the war, French and Ojibwe in the region worked for the independent North West Company. By the 1780s the fur-trading company controlled western Lake Superior and established Fort St. Louis at the mouth of the St. Louis River on what is now Conner's Point in Superior, Wisconsin; the post became the region's center of trade. Within ten years of the treaty signing, most Ojibwe had left Madeline Island for Wayekwaagichigamiing, which the French also called Fond du Lac, the name the Duluth neighborhood carries today.

Meanwhile, thirteen English colonies revolted, and when the gun smoke cleared they had created the United States of America. Benjamin Franklin helped negotiate terms for a second Treaty of Paris in 1783 on behalf of the newly minted Americans, including drawing boundaries. Initially, England was to control the entire north shore of Lake Superior. However, as historians have joked, Franklin's pencil slipped, and the line was drawn at the Pigeon River (today's border with Canada) and west to Lake of the Woods at the top center of the state. If it had not been for this adjustment, which was disputed for nearly sixty years, Duluth would be in Manitoba today.

Despite the treaty, the conflict between the United States and England continued, eventually erupting in the War of 1812. The American victory essentially ended European involvement in the US fur trade. Anticipating Europe's departure, in 1808 German immigrant John Jacob Astor formed the American Fur Company and established a modest trading post adjacent to the Ojibwe village at Fond du Lac. Astor took over the North West Company's interests in western Lake Superior in 1816, and a year later built a new, larger trading post at Fond du Lac. Fort St. Louis was abandoned, and the French and Ojibwe families in the trade began working for Astor.

The fur trade declined steeply in the 1830s as silk from China replaced beaver underfur as ideal hat-making material. An 1837 financial panic set off an economic depression, further damaging the industry. The American Fur Company failed in 1842, handing over its Fond du Lac post to the Missouri Fur Company, which abandoned it in 1847. While the fur trade had died, many French traders—particularly those who had married Ojibwe women—remained at Fond du Lac and throughout the region.

The American Fur Post at Fond du Lac as seen from Nekuk Island, long the site of an Ojibwe village, painted by James Otto Lewis to document the signing of the 1826 Treaty of Fond du Lac, which explains why American soldiers are camped outside the post's stockade.

Treaties and Reservations

Before its demise, the Fond du Lac fur post was the region's center of trade and consequently a natural location for large gatherings. In 1826 Michigan territorial governor William Cass and Colonel Thomas L. McKenney, the head of the newly formed United States Indian Department (USID), gathered Native leaders from throughout the region to the post to sign the first Treaty of Fond du Lac. Leaders of many northern Ojibwe bands agreed to the lines that had been drawn between Native nations as the result of an earlier treaty, and they granted the United States rights to mineral exploration and mining within Ojibwe lands in Michigan's Upper Peninsula and the northern halves of Wisconsin and Minnesota. In exchange, the Ojibwe at Sault Ste. Marie received a small annuity and the promise of a school. They did not surrender territory.

Michigan dispatched geologist Douglass Houghton to Lake Superior's south shore to find the copper everyone already knew was there.

The French had long noted the existence of copper deposits, and the Ojibwe believed that Lake Superior's Isle Royale—which they called Minong—and other islands were made of pure copper. Some explorers had actually seen the Ontonagon Boulder, 3,700 pounds of pure copper lying half-buried in the west branch of the Ontonagan River at the base of the Keweenaw Peninsula on what is now Michigan's Upper Peninsula (UP). Houghton mapped the peninsula in the 1830s and verified everyone's suspicions: the Keweenaw held vast copper deposits.

While the 1826 treaty allowed Americans to mine the copper, it did not allow them to take possession of the land. Following Houghton's report, the United States decided it wanted not simply to hold the mineral rights to the lands outlined in the 1826 treaty but to own them outright. And so in 1842 the USID invited representatives of the Lake Superior and Mississippi River Ojibwe to Madeline Island to discuss another treaty. By then, Treuer explains, the fur trade's decline had significantly diminished the Ojibwe's finances, and they were "willing to entertain any ideas that might buoy their economy." The meeting resulted in the first Treaty of La Pointe, in which the Ojibwe ceded the western half of Michigan's Upper Peninsula and northwestern Wisconsin, retaining reservations in their homelands.

Two months before the 1842 treaty signing, the United States and Britain finally settled their dispute over today's northeastern Minnesota, making the Grand Portage Ojibwe—who controlled Isle Royale—residents of what was then Michigan Territory, rather than British Canada. Government officials at La Pointe were not aware of this development until after the 1842 treaty was signed, so the Grand Portage Band was not involved in that agreement. In an 1844 amendment to the treaty, the Grand Portage Band ceded Isle Royale to the United States, and it became part of Michigan.

The mining began almost immediately, and from 1845 to 1887 the UP was the largest copper producer in the United States. The 1842 agreement also opened Lake Superior's south shore to whites; the Ojibwe were to continue living there, retaining "the right of hunting on the ceded territory, with the other usual privileges of occupancy, until required to remove by the President of the United States"—that is, until a reservation was set up for them.

At the lake's eastern end, the rapids of the St. Marys River between Lake Huron and Lake Superior had made it nearly impossible for large vessels to reach Lake Superior, as anything bigger than a canoe had to be hauled over land. Michigan had been unsuccessfully lobbying Congress for a canal-and-lock system to circumvent the rapids since the 1830s, but the copper trade put pressure on Washington to approve it. Finally, in 1852, Congress appropriated funds for the project, and in June 1855 the Soo Locks opened Lake Superior to shipping traffic.

The lake's north shore between today's Duluth and the Pigeon River at the US–Canada border was thought to hold as much, if not more, copper as Michigan's UP, and an 1847 government geologist's report indicated the shore held plenty of copper and likely a lot of iron as well.

In 1854 the USID again met with Ojibwe leaders at La Pointe to sign a treaty. Among those representing the Ojibwe was Kechewaishe of La Pointe, also known as Bizhiki, or Chief Buffalo. Bizhiki had been part of an excursion to Washington, DC, in 1852. The group did not like the earlier treaties, which would eventually force them to leave the region, and their protest of that provision led to the 1854 agreement. The treaty ceded to the United States land north and west of Lake Superior now making up Cook, Lake, St. Louis, and Carlton Counties. In exchange, the Ojibwe received some cash and equipment and, instead of being forced westward, established reservations within Ojibwe territory; they also retained hunting, fishing, and gathering rights. They included the Grand Portage Reservation (Gichionigamiing) at the Canadian border and the Fond du Lac Reservation (Nagaajiwanaang), located not at Wayekwaagichigamiing but farther up the St. Louis River in Carlton County, home to the Fond du Lac Band of Lake Superior Chippewa.

The ceded land included all of what would become Duluth except for a reserve of 682 acres—just over a square mile—negotiated by Bizhiki. Bizhiki chose land that would become the heart of Duluth, known later as the Buffalo Tract. The exact borders of this property have never been defined, though most accounts agree it was centered at Point of Rocks

Benjamin Armstrong, standing at right, and the five Ojibwe elders who traveled to Washington, DC, in 1852 to negotiate permanent homes for the Ojibwe once treaties forced them from their homes. Among them is Kechewaishe of La Pointe, also known as Chief Buffalo, Armstrong's father-in-law.

and included portions of today's Lincoln Park, Rice's Point, downtown and Canal Park business districts, and Central Hillside.

Bizhiki's descendants, however, were not to live on that land. Following his death in 1855, Bizhiki's son-in-law—trader Benjamin Armstrong—inherited the property. Armstrong is thought to have sold the land to a group of men in Ontonagon, Michigan, possibly to settle a debt. It was then subdivided and sold time and again. In the 1880s Frederick Prentice claimed he had purchased the land from Armstrong in the 1850s and began a series of lawsuits against those who owned parcels in the tract, demanding the return of his property. Prentice never won a single suit but he did profit, as historian Dwight Woodbridge

This sketch of Kay-be-sen-day-way-we-win of the Fond du Lac Chippewa was made ca. 1857 by Eastman Johnson.

explained: "[Duluthians] proved before the Supreme Court that this perennial nuisance was the hollowest of all 'fake' claims and effectually laid the Prentice bogy forever, not before, however, many lot owners had given up good sums of money to Mr. Prentice for quit claim deeds."

The Native American population in what is now Duluth began to decline once local Ojibwe began relocating to the Fond du Lac Reservation, roughly thirty-five miles west of Bizhiki's promised reserve. They would not enjoy sovereign land within the Buffalo Tract until the 1980s, and that would be limited to a casino in a former department store.

CHAPTER 2

At the Head of
the Lakes (1850–1869)

While the French referred to Lake Superior's far-western end as Fond du Lac (Bottom of the Lake), English-speaking explorers had an entirely different perspective. They called it the Head of the Lakes, a phrase later used to collectively identify Duluth and Superior, Wisconsin. The position of those communities on the opposite banks of the St. Louis River has tied them together physically, economically, and culturally; if not for the state line between them, Duluth and Superior would certainly have become one city. Consequently, their histories are profoundly intertwined.

Welcome to Superior City

In 1854 droves of immigrants began arriving at the Head of the Lakes, most from Michigan, Ohio, and New York, many aboard Great Lakes steamships that passed through the Soo Locks. That year surveyor George Riley Stuntz and others cut the Military Road from the convergence of the Mississippi and St. Croix Rivers to the St. Louis River dalles. In September speculators incorporated the Village of Superior, platting it between the Nemadji River and Conner's Point along the shore of Superior Bay behind both Wisconsin and Minnesota Points. Soon thereafter the Military Road was extended to Superior, and more immigrants began arriving by way of the road that winter, when frozen mud made for easier travel. The quickly built path was so rough that early resident Edmund Ely advised, "if you love your family, do not

"Just a Pile of Rocks"

Just a few Americans lived on the "Minnesota side" of Lake Superior prior to 1855, as it was illegal for anyone not licensed as a trader to live on unceded land. The most famous was Pennsylvanian George Riley Stuntz, primarily a government surveyor and considered by his white contemporaries to be the "first citizen" of both Duluth and Superior, who arrived in 1852 to survey the region. He began his work using a marker on Minnesota Point left by British surveyor Henry Bayfield in 1826, and he established a trading post and dock along Superior Bay. The only other non-Ojibwe residents of Minnesota Point were trading-post employees Charles Lord and R. H. Barrett and preemptor Harvey Fargo, who built a cabin near the post.

New Yorker Reuben Carlton—namesake of Minnesota's Carlton County—was already in what is now Duluth when Stuntz arrived, but he was far from the river's mouth. In 1847 the trader signed on to work as a blacksmith and farmer for the Ojibwe at Fond du Lac and established an eighty-acre farm just upstream from John Jacob Astor's former fur post.

Trader George Nettleton brought his bride, Julia, to the Head of the Lakes in 1853, establishing a trading post near the base of Minnesota Point. Like many early Duluthians, the Nettletons came from Ohio's Ashtabula County. When they first arrived, Julia later recalled, "There was no one in Superior at that time, and my husband said there must be a large city at the head of this lake some time. We couldn't tell whether it would be on the Minnesota side or on the Wisconsin side, but at that time there was nothing but a wilderness on the Superior shore. . . . Nothing—just a pile of rocks."

attempt to bring them over the Military Road." By the time a census was taken in April 1855, Superior was home to 385 people—291 men and boys and 93 women and girls including Pennsylvanians, New Englanders, and 64 "foreign-born." Those immigrants came from over a dozen countries, primarily Canada, England, Scotland, Ireland, and Germany. A year later the population had jumped to 585, including 329 men, 119 women, and 137 children. They called their village Superior City.

This lithograph by John Bachmann, a copy of a painting by Eastman Johnson, was published by P. S. Duval & Sons of Philadelphia in 1857 and depicts the view of the fledgling village of Superior, Wisconsin, in November 1856 as seen from George Stuntz's dock on Minnesota Point. The paddle wheeler shown is the *Lady Elgin*, which carried many pioneers of Superior and Duluth to the Head of the Lakes. *Library of Congress*

George R. Stuntz, pioneer surveyor, trader, road builder, railroad promoter, ore prospector, and "first citizen" of both Superior, Wisconsin, and Duluth, Minnesota. *Duluth Public Library*

The North Shore Copper Rush

Many of the same people who established the townsites that would become Duluth also came to the Head of the Lakes filled with dreams of striking it rich mining copper along Lake Superior's north shore. Beginning in 1856, many of them took the steamer *Seneca* from Superior to Buchanan, a brand-new townsite (named for presidential candidate James Buchanan) at the mouth of the Knife River twenty-four miles up the north shore from Minnesota Point. Leonidas Merritt, who arrived in Oneota in 1856 when he was twelve, later called Buchanan "the emporium of the North Shore, with a pretentious hotel . . . steamboat docks, several saloons, boarding houses, etc." The federal government established a land office at Buchanan, and there prospectors made claims on parcels of land along the Minnesota shores of Lake Superior from Duluth's modern borders to Grand Marais.

Those hoping to make fortunes mining copper plotted so-called copper towns, townsites that existed only on paper. Nearly all of them sat at the mouth of a river or stream, the same type of geological formations that yielded copper in Michigan. Most of these towns and their adjacent waterways were named for either the men who platted them or those they paid to "hold" the property by camping or building a small cabin on the site to protect it from claim jumpers.

Stretching north from what is now Duluth, copper towns established between 1856 and 1859 included Schmidt River (named for Henry Schmidt), Clifton near the Talmadge River (the latter named for claim-holder John Talmadge), Montezuma along the Sucker River, Stoney Point, Sucker Bay, Buchanan, Knife River, Burlington Bay (which later joined with Agate Bay to become Two Harbors), Flood Bay, Stewart River (named for John Stewart), Silver Creek, Encampment River (platted by George Stuntz), and Saxton (named for Superior and Duluth lighthouse-keeper Commodore Horace Saxton).

The exceptions along the north shore were Grand Marais, a trading outpost, and Beaver Bay, where the families of Christian Wieland, three of his brothers, and other German immigrants started a farming and logging community. The Wielands and their friends left their homeland to avoid mandatory military service established after the German revolution of 1848. They wasted no time looking for copper. Within weeks of their arrival they had built docks, a sawmill, and roads.

Some of the prospectors organized northeastern Minnesota's first mining outfit, the North Shore Mining Company. Daniel Cash, William Spalding, Samuel C. McQuade, William Kingsbury, Reuben Carlton, Vose Palmer, John Parry, and William Cowell pulled together an authorized capital of $400,000, worth over $11 million today. All they had to do was figure out which claims actually contained copper and then start mining.

But there was no copper there—at least not enough to justify opening a copper mine. None of the so-called copper towns contained much copper, and some none at all. In fact, very little copper was actually extracted from the North Shore. Most prospectors gave up following the Panic of 1857, abandoning all but Beaver Bay and Grand Marais.

The Townsites that Became Duluth

Many of these newcomers had their eyes on land across the bay and along the North Shore, where they hoped to become wealthy operating copper mines. Some couldn't wait for the signing of the second Treaty of La Pointe. One group, including Robert McLean, August Zachau, and Vose Palmer, quietly slipped out of Superior in a sailboat in the dead of night and made their way to the North Shore. There they began building a log cabin, but the effort came to a halt when those handling the axes refused to work until they were fed—an action McLean described as "the first labor strike at the Head of the Lakes." They never finished the cabin, but as soon as the treaty allowed, those would-be preemptors and many others swarmed the lake's Minnesota side, making legitimate claims and platting townsites, many of which would later form the City of Duluth.

Between today's Fortieth and Forty-Third Avenues East in Duluth, from the lakeshore to McCullough Street, James Bell platted the townsite of Bellville, but except for his cabin—which at least one historian believes was the same building started by Zachau and his friends in 1854—it remained unoccupied until the 1870s. Oregon and Chester Creeks (essentially Twenty-First and Fifteenth Avenues East) provided the borders for Captain James A. Markland's townsite of Endion (Ojibwe for "my, your, or his home"), which stretched from the lakeshore to about Fourth Street. West of Endion, the townsite of Portland covered the ground between Chester Creek and Third Avenue East from the lake to roughly Fifth Street. Its founders, including James D. Ray and Clinton Markell, hailed from Ashtabula, Ohio.

The newcomers established several townsites west of Portland in today's downtown Duluth, from roughly Fifth Street to Oatka (Ojibwe for "an opening") Beach on Minnesota Point near today's South Thirty-Eighth Street. George and William Nettleton, Joshua B. Culver, Orrin Rice, and Robert Jefferson staked out a townsite between Third Avenue East and Eighth Avenue West at the base of Point of Rocks, from First Street south to just above Buchanan Street in today's Canal Park business district. The Nettletons hosted a picnic on Minnesota Point in June 1856, asking their neighbors to suggest a name for their new town. After Reverend J. G. Smith regaled his fellow picnickers with heroic stories of Daniel Greysolon, Sieur du Lhut, they enthusiastically approved his anglicized suggestion of "Duluth." They anointed the choice with a champagne toast, confident their new town would become the "Queen of the West."

Directly above Duluth to Fifth Street John Pendergrast platted North Duluth, then lost nearly all of it in a dispute with the Nettletons. Immediately below Duluth to roughly today's ship canal William Cowell purchased property called Cowell's Addition, and south of that, all the way to Oatka, Markland and Robert Reed platted Middleton. Meanwhile C. P. Huestis and C. A. Post platted Fremont among the muck and floating islands below modern Michigan Street between Minnesota Point and Point of Rocks.

Those borders blurred in 1857, when the communities centered on and above Minnesota Point—including everything from Fifth Street to Oatka between Third Avenue East and Eight Avenue West—incorporated together as the town of Duluth.

West of Duluth Indian trader Orrin Rice established a post on his eponymously named point and operated a ferry service between it, Conner's Point, and Minnesota Point. Rice's Point townsite stretched from the point's southern end north to roughly Third Street, east to Point of Rocks, and west to Thirtieth Avenue West, including most of the West End (today's Lincoln Park).

A group composed mainly of Methodists established a townsite west of Rice's Point. They included Reverend Edmund Ely, a Massachusetts native and no stranger to the region. In the 1830s he had established a Protestant mission adjacent to the fur post at Fond du Lac, serving until 1839. Like many missionaries and traders, he was well positioned to join the land rush. He and his wife, Mary, returned to the Head of the Lakes after Minnesota was opened to whites. Ely convinced lumber mill engineer Henry Wheeler, a New Yorker working in St. Anthony Falls (later part of Minneapolis), to move to the Head of the Lakes and establish a sawmill at the townsite Ely had staked out near Forty-Second Avenue West. Ely also convinced another Methodist minister, James Peet, to join them. Nearby, Lewis Merritt and his son Napoleon—devout Methodists from Ashtabula—put in stakes of their own. Finding themselves like-minded and linked by religion, the Elys, Wheelers, Peets, Merritts, and others combined their claims and called their village Oneota, a derivation of Oneida, a tribe native to central New York. It stretched back from the bay to about Grand Avenue (which follows the same path as Third Street) roughly between Thirty-Third and Forty-Sixth Avenues West.

The land between Oneota and Fond du Lac remained undeveloped until the late 1880s. In the 1850s Fond du Lac was already home to many Ojibwe-and-French families who had remained after the fur post and mission closed, including that of Francis Roussain. Roussain—along with traders Reuben Carlton, Alexander Paul, George Morrison, and Joshua B. Culver—made it a village in 1856.

While these towns would eventually come together, evolving and expanding into today's Duluth, initially each hoped to be the center of a great city fueled by copper mining. But the copper rush proved to be a bust, and by the time the townsites of future Duluth were established, the North Shore prospectors had all but given up their dreams of cupric fortunes.

Panic and War

By the time the copper speculators stopped speculating, about 2,500 people lived in Superior and nearly 1,500 more had begun building homesteads from Endion to Oneota. Then came the Panic. In the 1850s, despite increasing development, the US economy was declining. Europe, home to many investors financing America's growth, also suffered from unstable economies. Banks powered western expansion by investing in railroads, but they were short on cash. In September 1857 worried investors hoped the California gold rush would rescue the United States. Indeed, the SS *Central America* was on its way to New York with thirty thousand pounds of gold, deposits of which would stabilize the nation's banks. Then, on September 12, the ship sank near Havana, Cuba, taking 425 lives—and the American economy—to the bottom of the Gulf of Mexico. The fallout was called the Panic of 1857.

The ensuing depression struck a considerable blow to the increasingly industrial North, hitting the Great Lakes region hard. In fact, while most of the country recovered within a year, towns along the lakes took longer. The farther west a community sat, the longer it took to recover. With no industry to support its population, people fled the Head of the Lakes in droves. James Bardon, who arrived in 1854, recalled that "lake steamers were overcrowded carrying people away," and by the time the Soo Locks closed for the shipping season, three-quarters of the population had left. Even George Nettleton abandoned his claims, and along with an army of others walked the Military Road to St. Paul.

Except for the town of Beaver Bay and a handful of hopeful copper prospectors, the North Shore was all but abandoned. A few stores remained open in Superior; none in the Minnesota townsites. No flour that first winter meant no bread. Those who remained fished and trapped and grew a few potatoes. Jerome Cooley, who moved to Duluth in 1873, would later refer to these hearty souls as the "Ancient and Honorable Order of the Fish Eaters." Local trade was handled on a barter system. When Orrin Rice offered to give two lots in Duluth to John Carey, St. Louis County's first judge, in exchange for a pair of boots, Carey refused—the footwear would be worth much more in the winter to come.

Sidney and Harriet Luce, farmers from Ashtabula County, Ohio, had arrived less than a year earlier. The Luces had been encouraged to invest in Portland by former neighbors who arrived before them, and they wanted to see their property. The Luces did not intend to stay, but when the panic struck and nearly everyone else fled, they remained to protect their investment and those of their friends.

Before the panic, Sidney Luce had built a wharf and a warehouse at the foot of Third Avenue East, the border between Portland and Duluth townsites and adjacent to the very spot at which Lake Superior's north shore met the base of Minnesota Point. Copper mining would certainly attract a railroad, Luce surmised, and a building boom along with it—and his facilities would be ready to receive the necessary supplies. The

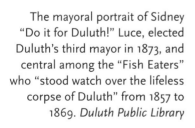

The mayoral portrait of Sidney "Do it for Duluth!" Luce, elected Duluth's third mayor in 1873, and central among the "Fish Eaters" who "stood watch over the lifeless corpse of Duluth" from 1857 to 1869. *Duluth Public Library*

copper bust and the panic forced Luce's building into a completely different role, described by the *Duluth Minnesotian* in 1873 as the "artery through which the pulsations of the coming city beat." Luce's warehouse, technically Duluth's first commercial building, became home to the Federal Land Office, the post office, and more. Carey called it the county's first courthouse as well as the home of the "register of deeds office, county auditor's and treasurer's office, annual township [*sic*] meetings, school district meetings, and other public and sometimes private meetings." The Luces lived on the top floor, which had one window.

Luce—whose motto was "Do it for Duluth!"—and others worked to retain the population, in part by creating jobs for unemployed men. In 1859 he staked German cooper Gottlieb Busch and three Yankee carpenters with land, lumber, and a brew kettle, and Busch began making beer along a stream they named Brewery Creek. The same year Henry Kiichli began brewing in Superior. Thanks to Luce, Busch, and Kiichli, even if those hanging on at the Head of the Lakes had only fish and potatoes to eat, at least they could wash them down with beer.

It would take a lot more than fermented hops to help Duluth and Superior survive. The 1860 census shows Douglas County with only 812 residents, down from 2,500 in Superior alone three years earlier. The St. Louis County townsites, home to 1,560 people in 1857, dropped to 406. That included 102 in Fond du Lac, 161 in Oneota, and just 80 in what the federal census bureau counted as Duluth: every settlement between and including Rice's Point and Endion. Ojibwe residents far outnumbered the immigrants, particularly in the summer; Luce noted that in August 1861, Minnesota Point was lined with camps housing hundreds of Ojibwe woman and children, as it was "the huckleberry season and they are very plentiful."

The Civil War further decimated the population, as Judge Carey later explained: "Many of those that yet remained departed, some with the patriotic spirit to enlist in the Union army . . . and others to their old homes in Canada (not being citizens)." Many prominent residents volunteered, including Joshua B. Culver. Sexagenarian Doras Martin had so much patriotic spirit he dyed his gray hair and whiskers black and lied about his age to fight for the Union.

During that period, historian Walter Van Brunt, who had moved to Duluth in 1869, would later write that "A few remained on duty at Superior, and George R. Stuntz, [William] Nettleton, [J. D.] Ray, [Horace] Saxton, [John] Carey, [Sidney] Luce, and [Luke] Marvin kept vigil over the lifeless corpse of Duluth."

Courting Mr. Cooke

Following the war some people returned to the Head of the Lakes while others did not. Even Reverend Ely had given up on Oneota. In 1865 Culver returned as a full colonel and built a sawmill on Minnesota Point. There were then just 294 people in all of St. Louis County—56 in Fond du Lac, 112 in Oneota, and 126 in Duluth.

Duluth enjoyed a brief boost in activity in what proved to be a false gold rush at Lake Vermilion ninety miles north of Duluth. Prospectors purchased gear, food, and lodging in Duluth before departing on the Vermilion Trail, also built by Stuntz. The road began near the Luce-Busch

Philadelphia financier Jay Cooke, whose investment in Duluth in the late 1860s set off a major boom period and gave Duluth the nickname "Jay Cooke's Town."
Duluth Public Library

brewery and followed an Ojibwe path north to Lake Vermillion, but the gold deposits never materialized.

Stuntz used his time near the lake to look for a less precious metal. North Albert Posey, a local blacksmith of Ojibwe descent, had shown Stuntz a chunk of iron ore two Ojibwe told him they had found near Lake Vermilion. While others looked for gold, Stuntz found iron. But when he returned to Duluth he had to put the idea of iron mining aside, as his friends needed his help luring a railroad.

St. Paul's William Banning chased a much more prudent dream than gold and copper mining. He and his fellow investors wanted to build a railroad from the Mississippi River to Lake Superior. Their Lake Superior & Mississippi Railroad (LS&M) would not only link two great waterways, becoming a very busy "portage" railway, but it would also connect to the eastern terminus of the Northern Pacific Railroad (NP), recently authorized to run from the Head of the Lakes to the Pacific Ocean at Puget Sound. But Banning and his friends ran out of money after building just a few miles of track.

They turned to Philadelphia financier Jay Cooke. Cooke's banking house had financed much of the Union Army's effort during the Civil War, selling bonds to wealthy Europeans. Cooke, who was also being courted by the Northern Pacific's investors, came to Banning's rescue, providing financing that secured the LS&M's future. But the railroad's northern terminus hadn't been determined.

Both Superior and Duluth wanted the railroad, as it would surely make its host city a great shipping center, eclipsing Chicago. Superiorites assumed their town was a lock. They had financial backing from the East and geography was on their side. The Superior Entry between Minnesota and Wisconsin Points—the conduit through which shipping traffic flowed between the lake and the St. Louis River—was directly adjacent to Superior and seven miles from Duluth's center. And it would be much easier to build a railroad on Superior's flat, marshy land than on the narrow pile of rocks across the bay. Banning warned Duluthians in an 1867 letter that Superior's backers had been "circulating rumors that it is not possible to find room on the North Shore either on the lake or bays, to build a railroad, lay out and build a town, or do any kind of commercial business."

Cooke visited the Head of the Lakes in June 1868, according to the *St. Paul Daily Press*, "on business connected with the eastern terminus" of the LS&M and to see for himself timber property he had purchased along the lower St. Louis, Nemadji, and Cloquet Rivers. It included land along the St. Louis River dalles, which he envisioned powering a hydroelectric dam above Fond du Lac. During his trip Cooke met with Luce, Culver, and other Duluth leaders, and even got in a little fishing on the Lester River, but reportedly "never got a bite."

Since Cooke held the LS&M's purse strings, the townsite's leaders needed to persuade him to terminate the railroad in Duluth. Culver and company apparently failed to convince Cooke to choose Duluth during his visit—and that's where Stuntz came in. Stuntz's old boss, former surveyor general of the United States George Sargent, had spent the war selling bonds for Cooke. Sargent had sent Stuntz to the Head of the Lakes in 1852, and four years later told his fellow Bostonians that "the undeveloped wealth of the Lake Superior region offers reward beyond calculation to those who have the energy and enterprise to secure it." With an introduction from Sargent, Stuntz would try to convince Cooke to bring the LS&M to Duluth. So the surveyor traveled east in January 1869. Sargent not only made the introduction but also purchased twenty lots in Duluth, sight unseen.

In Philadelphia, Stuntz assured Cooke the land along his railroads could be sold to farmers at a healthy profit. He also mentioned northeastern Minnesota's potential mineral and timber resources and Sargent's real-estate investment. Shortly after Stuntz's visit, Cooke selected Duluth as the LS&M's northern terminus. Stuntz's visit also ultimately helped convince Cooke to invest in the NP, construction of which would begin near today's Carlton, Minnesota, heading west. There it would connect with the LS&M and run to Lake Superior, making Duluth the NP's eastern terminus.

Cooke's choice is arguably the most significant moment in Duluth's history. Van Brunt later described the transformation that followed as nothing short of miraculous: "A glorious resurrection took place; the lifeless corpse [of Duluth], touched by the wand of Jay Cooke, sprang full-armed from the tomb." Cooke's investment would not only bring the Minnesota townsite back to life but also forever tip the scales in Duluth's favor over Superior, leading to decades of conflict between the two communities.

CHAPTER 3

Boom to Bust (1869–1877)

What Jay Cooke waved was less a wand than it was a wad of cash. By May 1869 his agents had arrived in Duluth and began spending his money as well as that of his associate E. W. Clark. Those agents—George Sargent, George C. Stone, and Luther Mendenhall—would become prominent figures in Duluth's history. They opened the town's first bank, which everyone called Jay Cooke's Bank. They built one of Duluth's first hotels, the Clark House, named for Clark. They financed the construction of Duluth's first church building, named St. Paul's Episcopal Church after Cooke's home parish in Cheltenham, Pennsylvania—locals called it Jay Cooke's Church. They spent not only Cooke's and Clark's money but their own as well, investing in early businesses. Eastern newspapers called Duluth Jay Cooke's Town.

Newcomers

Cooke's men weren't the only newcomers. The population began growing dramatically after Cooke announced his railroad terminus decision. Some had come for the gold rush and stayed, too broke to leave. Others came to get in on the ground floor. They included Colonel Charles Graves of Massachusetts, a Union Army veteran who would become a civic, political, and business leader, as well as Connecticut native Roger Munger, who left a successful business in St. Paul to move to Duluth in early 1869 where he and his wife, Olive, became, as he later described, one of "fourteen families . . . all gathered together in a little hamlet at

First Impressions of Fledgling Duluth

In August 1869 journalist John Trowbridge visited Duluth as part of an excursion group chiefly made up of Lake Superior & Mississippi Railroad investors, including Jay Cooke's brother Pitt. From St. Paul they took a train on the LS&M as far north as it was built—fifty miles—at which point horse-drawn coaches carried them over the bruising and muddy Military Road to a point four miles south of Carlton, where they turned toward the village of Fond du Lac. There they boarded two steamships and headed down the St. Louis River to Duluth. Trowbridge's lofty description of the nascent community appeared in *Atlantic* magazine the following year. Here are his first impressions of the Head of the Lakes after his party departed Fond du Lac:

> As the two little steamers found their way out from among the windings of the St. Louis River (where half the time one boat appeared, to those on board the other, to be gliding about, not on any stream, but breast-deep in a grassy sea of flat meadows), and desperately puffing and panting, put their noses into the white teeth of an easterly gale on St. Louis Bay, a bleak cluster of new-looking wooden houses, on a southward-fronting hillside, was pointed out to us as the Mecca of our pilgrimage.
>
> The first sight, to us shivering on deck, was not particularly cheering. But as we passed on into Superior Bay, and a stroke of light from a rift in the clouds fell like a prophetic finger on the little checkered spot brightening in the wilderness, the view became more interesting. The town lies on the lower terraces of wooded hills which rise from the water's edge, by easy grades, to the distant background of a magnificent mountain range—a truly imposing site, to one who can look beyond those cheap wooden frames—the staging whereby the real city is built—and see the civilization of the future clustering along the shore, and hanging upon the benches of that ample amphitheater.
>
> The two bays were evidently once an open basin of the lake, from which they have been cut off, one after the other, by points of land formed by the action of its waves meeting the current of the river. Between the lake and

bay is Minnesota Point—an enormous bar seven miles in length, covered by a long procession of trees and bushes, which appear to be marching in solid column, after their captain, the lighthouse, across the head of the lake, towards the land of Wisconsin. It is like a mighty arm thrust down from the north shore to take the fury of the lake storms on one side, and to protect the haven thus formed on the other. Seated on the rocky shoulder of this arm, with one foot on the lake, and the other on the bay, is the infant city of Duluth. . . .

Situated at the western extremity of the grandest lake and river chain in the world—that vast freshwater Mediterranean which reaches from the Gulf of St. Lawrence almost to the center of North America—it required no great degree of sagacity to perceive that here was to be the key to the quarter of the hemisphere—or hereabouts. Wherever was established the practical head of navigation between the northern range of States and the vastly more extensive undeveloped region beyond, there must be another and perhaps even a greater Chicago.

the base of Minnesota Point." Graves, Munger, and others like them invested in just about every enterprise they could think to organize.

Another 1868 newcomer was Dr. Thomas Foster, a self-taught journalist and physician who moved his *Minnesotian* newspaper from St. Paul to Duluth after Culver and others offered him a free building. In 1868 Foster gave a grand oration during an Independence Day celebration on Minnesota Point, boasting of the future Duluth. His speech, which appeared in the *Minnesotian*'s inaugural issue in April 1869, described a network of rail lines that would transform the townsite into a mecca for commerce, when, from the Atlantic to the Pacific, "all roads would lead to Duluth . . . our Zenith City of the Unsalted Seas"—a nickname Duluthians still use proudly today.

The spring of 1869 brought the arrival of immigrants, mostly Scandinavians, recruited to help build the railroads with the promise of inexpensive farmland. Railroad laborers also included about three hundred young men from Philadelphia's slums who had followed Cooke's money west. The Fish Eaters called the newcomers Sixty-Niners, and by midsummer they had swelled the town's population to over two thousand. Construction of the LS&M west from Duluth began on May 4, 1869. The railroad built docks, a warehouse, and a freight depot along the lakeshore at the foot of Third Avenue East—directly in front of Luce's warehouse—to transfer cargo between train cars and vessels.

A City Is Born

In 1869 journalist John Trowbridge wrote that "civilization is attracted to the line of a railroad like steel-filings to a magnet; and [Duluth] appears to be the point of a magnet of more than ordinary power." Indeed, by early 1870 Duluth's population exceeded 3,100. Most were immigrants, over a third of them Swedish. Norwegians made up 13 percent, about the same portion as recently arrived Germans, Irish, and Canadians. A bill passed by the Minnesota State Legislature on March 6 made the

The groundbreaking ceremony for the Northern Pacific Railroad, February 15, 1870. At the center is *Duluth Minnesotian* publisher Dr. Thomas Foster, who first called Duluth the "Zenith City of the Unsalted Seas." He is surrounded by Duluth pioneers including Joshua B. Culver, William Nettleton, Luke Marvin, Clinton Markell, Sidney Luce, James D. Ray, and others he would later vilify as members of "the Ring." *UMD Martin Library*

town of Duluth—officially including newly annexed Endion, Portland, and Rice's Point—the City of Duluth.

Until this boom, more Ojibwe populated Duluth than did whites. While all lived peacefully together, the Ojibwe were often feared by newly arrived European immigrants, an attitude fueled primarily by portrayals of Native Americans as savages in newspapers and books. Ojibwe were further marginalized by whites who refused to hire them for labor, relying instead on European immigrants. Consequently, the Ojibwe population declined dramatically over the years, as many relocated to reservations or became assimilated by marriage.

By the time Duluth became a city its newcomers had already caused some trouble. Many of the "Philadelphia Roughs" spent more time drinking than working, a factor which led to the community's first murder. Meanwhile Dr. Foster, brought to Duluth to herald its achievements, had become highly critical of his benefactors. He had come to consider many of them members of what he called "the Ring," a group that included the city's founders, a few well-heeled Sixty-Niners, Cooke's agents, and LS&M investors.

Foster's dislike for the Ring came from two simple issues: he felt they unfairly "ran" the community, and several were Democrats. Foster had helped organize Minnesota's Republican Party and was instrumental to its Duluth founding. On March 19 his newspaper suggested the group would assume total control of Duluth "if the people were fool enough to let them succeed." Foster failed to recognize that political affiliation mattered little to Duluth's early power brokers, as Ring members ran for office on both tickets. Culver, William Nettleton, and George Stone ran as Democrats; Sidney and Orlando Luce and Roger Munger as Republicans.

Duluth held its first election on April 4, 1870. The Zenith City adapted a mayor-council system of government in which a common council, made up of two aldermen representing each of the city's wards, advised a mayor who served only a one-year term but wielded considerable power, including appointing unelected city officials without council approval. Town-founder Joshua B. Culver was elected mayor; Cooke agent George Stone, treasurer; Fish Eater Orlando Luce, comptroller; and Sixty-Niner Walter Van Brunt, city clerk. Aldermen included Sidney Luce, Roger Munger, William Nettleton, James D. Ray, William Spalding, Luke Marvin, and Nick Decker, who had purchased the Luce-Busch brewery. Foster's report on the election accused Ring supporters of bribing voters with cash and whiskey.

The Ring would indeed run Duluth during its first few years. Clinton Markell succeed Culver as mayor, followed by Sidney Luce, who won office while out of town and unaware of his nomination. Ring associates served as trustees of Duluth's first churches and sat on its first school board. They organized the city's first chamber of commerce and either lured industrial enterprises to town or organized and built them themselves: sawmills, coal docks, merchandise docks, grain terminals—even a factory to make railcars for Cooke's railroads and a blast furnace to supply the plant with steel. For the next twenty years these men essentially competed to see who could contribute most to the city's development, and to their own fortunes along the way.

The Ring quickly lost patience with Foster's abrasive and challenging approach to journalism, which leaned heavily on personal rants and rarely offered unbiased reporting. As Van Brunt later wrote, Duluth's city fathers had "tired of [Foster], as he had become too arrogant and dictatorial and entirely too obstreperous . . . and they concluded that they must and would have another paper."

On Cooke's advice the Ring approached Robert Mitchell of the *Superior Tribune*. Mitchell had arrived in Superior ten months earlier, leasing the facilities of the *Superior Gazette* from its former publisher's widow. Van Brunt recalled that he and others "entered into secret negotiations to bring Mitchell and his paper over to Duluth." On April 23, 1870, they used a barge and the cover of darkness to move the *Tribune* across the bay: "Quickly and quietly, at dead of night, we took Mitchell and his outfit, including cases [of type—which Mitchell didn't own], to Duluth."

Foster literally lost his monopoly overnight, and for the next two years he filled his columns with cheap shots at Mitchell and his benefactors. The doctor's anger was nothing compared to that of the Superiorites, already bruised and bitter about losing their railroads to those "cliff dwellers" across the bay. Mitchell later recalled that the move "incensed the people of Superior, owing to the intensely bitter feeling then existing there towards Duluth; in those days the man from Superior who would cast his lot with Duluth was regarded as a traitor to Superior."

While Foster fumed, Duluth boomed. More immigrants poured in to build the railroads. Loggers clear-cut the city's hillside, defining its streets and providing timber that Culver's and Munger's sawmills cut into the lumber that became the city's first houses, churches, docks, and warehouses. Duluth's Minnesota neighbors joined in the prosperity: the Oneota sawmill also cut boards for buildings, and its nearby brickyard made the material to face them; three quarries in Fond du Lac stayed busy providing brownstone for foundations and trim. In the summer of 1870 LS&M director William Branch and friends financed Branch's Hall, Duluth's first brick building, at 416 East Superior Street. The LS&M was completed in August, after which daily train service shifted the city into another gear. Grain from St. Paul began arriving by the trainload, loaded onto vessels at the LS&M docks and shipped east to mills along the Great Lakes.

Not that everything ran smoothly. In May of 1870 newly appointed police chief Robert Bruce skipped town owing creditors about $3,000—worth over $60,000 today—and was never heard from again. The city's wooden fire hall burned to the ground in October 1871, just months after the volunteer fire department obtained its first engine, which was destroyed in the conflagration.

Meanwhile, travelers flocked to the comfort of the railroad, all but abandoning the Military Road, and commerce bypassed Superior. Since Duluth's business district sat seven miles from the Superior Entry, the city built an outer harbor. Mayor Culver financed the construction of Citizen's Dock, a municipal wharf for commercial and passenger vessels

The northwest corner of Lake Superior photographed in 1871, showing a
locomotive of the LS&M railroad, the railroad's freight depot, grain elevator A,
and the breakwater. *Lake Superior Railroad Museum*

extending into the lake from Morse Street. East of the railroad's facilities
along the lake between Third and Fourth Avenues East, Munger and
Markell began building grain elevator A, financed by the LS&M.

A Canal Is Dug

Exposed at the very northwestern tip of Lake Superior, Duluth's outer
harbor did not provide adequate safety from Lake Superior's often-
stormy seas. Crews constructed a wooden breakwater extending into
the lake adjacent to the grain elevator, but the structure itself kept
breaking. The need for a safe harbor revived a plan first considered
in the 1850s: dig a canal through Minnesota Point, allowing vessels to
find calm water behind the sandbar. City leaders couldn't have chosen
a more symbolic place to position the canal: along the path of Portage

Street, which itself followed Onigamiinsing, the Native portage du Lhut had supposedly crossed 191 years earlier. For centuries the Dakota, Ojibwe, and fur traders had used the path for the same reason Duluth was digging the canal: to bypass the Superior Entry.

Cooke financed the operation, lending the city $50,000 from the LS&M's coffers in the form of one hundred $500 bonds bearing seven percent interest, with final payment due in 1890. The city hired W. W. Williams and Co., which sent the dredging tug *Ishpeming* to Duluth. The *Ishpeming's* steam shovel took its first bite out of Minnesota Point on September 5, 1870, and chewed up sand and gravel until mid-November, when the ground froze.

The dredger returned to work on April 24, 1871, digging continuously during daylight hours until Saturday, April 29. By then she had cut a swath thirty feet wide and eight feet deep to within a few feet of the lake side when, the *Minnesotian* reported, her shovel struck a vein of impenetrably frozen gravel. A group of "determined" men quickly assembled and with "shovels and picks and drills and powder (two kegs)" they scooped, smashed, bored, and blasted through the rock, allowing the *Ishpeming* to continue her work. At 1 PM that day the first cut was complete, connecting the lake and river within Duluth's borders—or, in the words of the often-verbose Dr. Foster, "the union of the waters became forthwith an accomplished fact."

That summer the Northern Pacific Railroad began constructing docks, wharves, and a rail line on the swampy land between Minnesota Point and Rice's Point above the canal site, creating a massive commercial district. Once the canal and NP facilities were complete, the only thing in the way of Duluth's future success was its neighbor across the bay—and Superior's citizens were not happy.

Superior was then smarting from yet another blow to its future. Three months before the canal was complete, Kentucky representative J. Proctor Knott delivered a scathing speech to Congress designed to scuttle a massive land grant proposed for a railroad between Hudson, Wisconsin, on the St. Croix River to Superior and Bayfield on Lake Superior's South Shore. But he confused Superior with the Zenith

Duluth's Defining Creation Myth

The initial digging of Duluth's ship canal was fairly simple, and researchers have traced its progress through reports published in the *Duluth Minnesotian* and the *Duluth Morning Call*. The steam-powered dredging tug *Ishpeming* began cutting through Minnesota Point in September 1870, stopped when the ground froze in November, and started again in late April 1871, finishing on April 29.

Over the years those events have evolved into an extraordinarily tall tale that many still believe. Several versions of the legend exist, and most go something like this:

In January 1871 Superiorites uncovered Duluth's plot to dig a canal (in the legends, the digging had not yet begun), which would reduce shipping traffic to Superior. Superior's leaders filed for an injunction to stop the dredging, which the courts granted in April. A telegram received on Friday, April 28, warned Duluthians that a government-dispatched courier was in route to deliver the injunction. So the call went out for every able-bodied man, woman, and child in town "who could handle a spade or shovel, or beg, borrow, or steal a bucket or a bushel basket" to converge on the canal site where they "dug, scratched, and burrowed 'till it was finished." By the break of dawn Monday, they had cleared a canal. The courier arrived at the exact moment the tug *Frank C. Fero* passed through the canal. Recognizing the hand-dug ditch as a navigable waterway, the courier decided then and there that the injunction had been rendered invalid and immediately tore up the document, ending the whole affair.

Some versions have the *Ishpeming* cutting the entire canal in two days. Many claim the courier arrived on horseback while others say he took the train. In perhaps the tallest version of the tale, recorded by the *Duluth Evening Herald* in 1929, the canal was created with one perfectly executed explosion: "Leading Duluthians of the time . . . led by [William] Sargent . . . formed the 'Dynamite Club.' Under the cover of darkness . . . bankers, clerks, professional men and laborers worked frantically with pick and shovel. . . . As daylight approached and they realized they would not finish the task, leaders called for dynamite. . . . When the debris settled the dynamiters were rewarded by the water rushing through the ditch thus created."

This story fails to consider that William Sargent was only eleven years old at the time. So how did these tales take root? Like all good myths, they contain some truth: a little hand digging and a couple kegs of blasting powder were used to break up a stubborn patch of frozen gravel on April 29. There was an injunction, but it did not arrive until nearly a week after the *Ishpeming* had finished its initial cut. The lawsuits dragged on until 1877, but never interfered with the canal's operation.

The legends likely started as elaborations of true events told time and again, becoming canonical after they were set into type. The first version of the story found in print—including the "dug, scratched, and burrowed" passage—comes from British author James Howard Bridge's 1888 book *Uncle Sam at Home*. Roger Munger and his family told versions of the legend to newspaper reporters beginning in the 1890s, and it was reprinted when he died in 1913. His recollection appeared in his son-in-law Dwight Woodbridge's 1910 history of Duluth: "I was engaged by the citizens of Duluth to dig the channel. We began work on a Saturday and by night Superior knew what we were about. At once the people over there began to scurry around to get a federal injunction restraining us. I hired a gang of several hundred men . . . and we worked all that day and far into the night. . . . When the Superior people came over Monday morning there was the channel open and they couldn't do anything."

Perhaps the stories perpetuate because people just can't resist telling them, facts be damned. Munger himself helped hire the *Ishpeming*— he knew full well his account was a fib. Bridge was fourteen years old in 1870 and did not live in the United States, let alone Duluth. Jerome Cooley, who moved to Duluth in 1873, recorded his version in a 1922 book of his "recollections." Otto Wieland, born in 1871, told his tale to the Works Project Administration in 1942. The *Minneapolis Tribune* featured its account in 1945. Duluth teacher Dora Mary MacDonald retold it in her 1949 book *This Is Duluth*, researched in part by her elementary school students. Even today several websites present the myth as fact.

Despite the tallness of the tale, the legend reinforces a central theme of Duluth's formative years: the determined self-sufficiency of its founding generation, who never backed away from a challenge and stood up to confront every obstacle they encountered.

The dredge *Ishpeming* (left) cutting the Duluth Ship Canal in April 1871. *Lake Superior Maritime Collection*

City, titling his speech "The Untold Delights of Duluth" and lacing it with what were then considered humorous barbs. ("I have always been under the impression . . . that in the region around Lake Superior it was cold enough for at least nine months in the year to freeze the smoke-stack off a locomotive. But . . . Duluth must be a place of untold delights, a terrestrial paradise, fanned by the balmy zephyrs of an eternal spring, clothed in the gorgeous sheen of ever-blooming flowers, and vocal with the silvery melody of nature's choicest songsters.") Knott's colleagues interrupted him sixty-two times with "roars of laughter." But while the speech made Duluth a laughingstock, it ended Superior's chance for its own railroad.

Superior's leaders recognized that once Duluth had both the rail-road and a canal, shipping traffic to the Wisconsin city would all but cease—as would hopes for its future. But Superiorites couldn't argue against Duluth's right to improve its own infrastructure, unless they could prove that the canal would irreparably harm Superior. So they developed an argument: the canal would divert the St. Louis River's current, depositing silt at the Superior Entry rather than farther out into the lake as it normally did, thereby blocking navigation through the entry and reducing commerce in Superior.

On April 24, 1871, an injunction was filed against Duluth and the dredging company to "be enjoined and restrained from constructing said canal." However, Duluth could keep its canal if it also built a dike between Minnesota and Rice's Points to guide the river's currents through the natural entry. It was the first of several lawsuits that kept lawyers on both sides of the bay busy for the next six years. The dike cost Duluth nearly $100,000, two men died building it, and saboteurs tried to blow it up. Cutting off the current also cut off trade between Duluth and Superior, further injuring Superior but not Duluth. Superior then sued Duluth to remove the dike. Never built to withstand the river's currents, the structure eventually broke apart on its own.

The NP offered a resolution in March 1873. If Wisconsin would drop its lawsuits, the railroad promised to construct a line between Rice's and Conner's Points and along Superior's shoreline all the way to the Nemadji River and build a grain elevator as well, essentially leveling the infrastructural playing field. It looked like Duluth and Superior had found a way to come together, the St. Louis River having demonstrated that it was folly to try to keep them apart. By the summer of 1873 the canal bustled with shipping traffic while Superiorites eagerly awaited their railroad. Vespasian Smith, an Ohio physician, became mayor of Duluth—Luce had resigned in February, returning to Ohio to run the family farm. Dr. Smith, despite running unopposed, was elected with one vote cast against him—and he claimed it was his own. The new mayor oversaw a population of roughly five thousand.

And then Jay Cooke ran out of money.

A Fortune Is Lost

Following the Civil War, Cooke and others had overinvested in railroads. In 1873 the Philadelphia financier was expecting a federal loan of $300 million—about $6.5 billion today—but rumors that his bank had

Duluth photographed in 1873, just before Jay Cooke's—and consequently the city's—financial collapse. Note the ship canal's piers jutting out into Lake Superior at left and the dredges at right. *MNHS Collections*

no credit torpedoed the transaction, forcing him into bankruptcy on September 18. Other banks soon followed suit, setting off the Panic of 1873, the beginning of an economic malaise that lasted six years. Within two years 110 railroads failed and 18,000 US businesses closed.

The depression even affected European economies, but few communities were hit harder than Duluth. Financed either directly or indirectly by Cooke's enterprises, nearly half of the city's businesses disappeared within two months. As in 1857, people fled in flocks. Van Brunt reports that one resident remembered Duluth's population dropping to "1,300 souls" by the middle of 1874. More reliable sources estimate it at 2,500— half the pre-panic number. Even Dr. Foster was gone, having abandoned his Zenith City two years earlier, leaving the *Minnesotian* to his sons, who later sold it to his rival, Mitchell.

By then Duluth and Superior were again sparring over the canal. After Cooke's bankruptcy the NP had failed and was undergoing reorganization, leaving no money to build Superior's promised infrastructure.

The Wisconsin town felt it was within its rights to seek reparation and had clear evidence that the lack of a railroad had cost it commerce: in 1874, while 290 commercial ships called on the port of Duluth—moving tons of grain, coal, and other goods—not a single vessel passed through the Superior Entry. Wisconsin began filing lawsuits that December.

The canal dispute was just one of Duluth's problems. The LS&M had also fallen into receivership, and plans for its reorganization had yet to materialize. And while the exodus had slowed, the city's population continued to drop. Those who remained held out hope that once the Red River Valley along the Minnesota–Dakota Territory border blossomed with wheat and other grains, Duluth—with its railroads, grain terminals, ship canal, and both outer and inner harbors—had the infrastructure in place to turn itself into the major shipping center its forefathers had foreseen. If it could just hold on until then.

CHAPTER 4

Bust to Boom (1877–1887)

Dr. Vespasian Smith, "a staunch, sterling old character that builded well with his great common sense," was reelected in 1874, this time by three votes ("I made two enemies," he reportedly said). While Smith was credited for his ability to keep Duluthians "thinking sensibly," he did not run for reelection in 1875. That year Peter Dean, a dry-goods merchant from New York, ran on an idea that many of the city's founders did not find sensible: repudiation, essentially disputing the validity of a contract and refusing to honor its terms—a tactic used to reconstruct southern states following the Civil War. Dean suggested Duluth simply default on its debt, clearing its books while simultaneously wiping its creditors' investments—but many of those bond owners were the city's civic and business leaders. Described as a "bluff and gruff and hearty" man who loved Duluth, Dean won the election but couldn't sell his idea to the city council. Van Brunt called Dean's time in office "dark days indeed; business was at a standstill; no one had money with which to pay taxes; city debts were unpaid; interest on the bonded indebtedness was permitted to run on." The 1875 census found 2,415 people struggling to make a living in the Zenith City, with another 110 in Oneota and 125 more in Fond du Lac doing little better.

A City No More

When tailor "Uncle John" Drew replaced Dean as mayor in 1876, he and others recognized that while repudiation was not the answer to

Duluth's economic problems, it would take an equally bold move to pull the city out of the financial muck. Meanwhile, the city owed a lot of money to its bondholders—about $500,000 not including interest by one estimate, more than $12 million today. Drew and the city aldermen, treasurer, and comptroller who advised him decided that to rebuild Duluth's financial house, they first had to burn most of it down.

With the council's consent, district court judge Ozora P. Stearns created legislation to reorganize Duluth as a village and compound its debt, reissuing its bonds at twenty-five cents on the dollar. To ensure the village remained motivated to pay off the remainder, its borders were retracted to its First and Second Wards—between Fourth Avenue West and Third Avenue East from Fifth Street to Oatka Beach. As the village paid off its debt, Woodbridge explained, it would "take in more and more of the city in proportion to the amount of her indebtedness paid."

The legislation passed, making city leaders both happy and anxious, as they feared retribution in the form of lawsuits brought by angry bondholders, who essentially lost 75 percent of their investment. At the final city council meeting in March 1877, city fathers set fire to a stack of cancelled bonds—an act Woodbridge described as "a burnt offering." Stearns became receiver of the new debt, and the City of Duluth existed no more.

But it wasn't a village yet. By the legislation's design the community first became the District of Duluth, allowing city officials to resign their elected positions and thereby disconnect themselves from any debt-related legal battles brought against the village. They did so immediately. In October the district gave way to the Village of Duluth, whose chief executive would hold the title of president; Danish lumberman and brownstone-quarry owner Andreas M. Miller was its first.

The reorganization also essentially ended the canal dispute with Superior. Following the Panic of '73 the federal government had spent $10,000 improving the canal. While presiding over Wisconsin's latest lawsuit in 1877, Judge Samuel F. Miller noted that by virtue of its financial investment, the federal government—which had approved of the canal's construction—had also essentially "taken possession and control of the work" on the canal. He declared that Wisconsin had no right to interfere in the operation of a federal facility.

And that was the end of that—for Duluth, at least. The decision stung Superiorites for years, as James Bardon recalled decades later: "When Duluth had a railroad and Superior had none, when Duluth had business and commerce and Superior had none, it was hard to keep still and Wisconsin raised questions on the canal, etc., and kept a belligerent attitude now happily ended."

Up from the Ashes

Duluth perfectly timed its restructuring. Within a year after the Zenith City was reduced to a village, farmers in the Red River Valley began sending wheat and other grains east on the reorganized Northern Pacific Railroad. For the next three years they sent an average of 1.7 million bushels of wheat to Duluth to be shipped to mills along the Great Lakes. Starting in 1878, as Duluth's post-panic population bottomed out at 2,200, grain elevators began popping up on Rice's Point and adjacent to elevator A on the outer waterfront.

Together with the ship canal, the Northern Pacific Railroad, whose tracks are seen in the foreground, and the row of grain elevators jutting out from Rice's Point were paramount to Duluth's economic recovery in the 1880s. *Duluth Public Library*

More than grain began passing through the port. Since 1871 Duluth had been supplying coal, most of it mined in Pennsylvania and Ohio, to Minneapolis and St. Paul. In 1875 Northwestern Fuel had built the city's first dedicated coal dock. By 1880 coal docks stretched among the elevators along Rice's Point's eastern shore. The St. Paul & Duluth Railroad—the reorganization of the Lake Superior & Mississippi Railroad—and the Northern Pacific Railroad helped Duluth ship coal to cities in eight states.

Much of the coal remained in the Zenith City, keeping homes and buildings warm and fueling the furnaces of steam-powered grain elevators and lumber mills. Most of these facilities had their own dedicated coal docks, and several sawmills went to work along the western shore of Rice's Point and the riverbank west of it. The lumber industry, played out in Michigan and nearing exhaustion in northwestern Wisconsin, was working its way to the pine forests of northeastern Minnesota, and within a few years lumber mills would line the St. Louis River from Rice's Point to Grassy Point. More coal fueled the blast furnace, dormant since 1874, which was reignited in 1880 as well.

The 1880 census recorded the population at 3,483, further demonstrating the village's return to prosperity. Miller had passed the presidential baton to former mayor Drew in 1879, who in turn handed it back to former mayor Dean a year later. Under Dean the village paid off a large portion of its debt, and after Stearns set fire to another $5,000 worth of bonds, the mayor resigned midterm. St. Louis county attorney Josiah D. Ensign stepped in to take his place and was easily reelected in January 1881. That April the village went through yet another reorganization and began to regain more of its former shape. A new charter restructured the government to behave more like a city than a business, returning to a system led by a mayor advised by a council of aldermen. Ensign won an uncontested mayoral race, and the village boundaries were pushed west to Thirtieth Avenue West, including all of Rice's Point, and east to roughly Eighth Avenue East along Brewery Creek.

But just as Duluth was stitching itself back together, another portion of the original city split off. In the 1877 reorganization, the strip of Minnesota Point below the canal had become the village's First

Ward, but its citizens felt disenfranchised. Landowners had seen their property values nose-dive after the canal turned their portion of the point into an island. Each year since they had lobbied for a permanent bridge over the canal, but civic leaders had ignored them. So in 1881 the community ceded from Duluth and organized itself as the Village of Park Point.

By 1881 Duluth's population had climbed to 7,800 and so much grain passed through the village that its business leaders organized the Duluth Board of Trade to set and regulate grain prices. Founding members included some familiar names, including Charles Graves, Walter Van Brunt, Roger Munger, and Clinton Markell. The grain industry boomed throughout the 1880s. Four years after the board's formation, Duluth boasted fourteen grain elevators, eleven of them along Rice's Point.

That year Graves and Van Brunt installed Duluth's first telephone system, and the next year Graves replaced Ensign as mayor. Members of the city's old guard kept taking turns as mayor, as Joshua B. Culver returned to the office in 1883, the year the Duluth Street Railway Company began operating a mule-driven streetcar service along Superior Street between Third Avenue East and Eighth Avenue West. Culver died while visiting New York in July, and Graves served out his term. By then the population had jumped to fourteen thousand, nearly doubling in two years.

As 1883 gave way to 1884, Ensign once again sat in the mayor's chair, overseeing some 16,690 citizens, many of them buzzing about the opening of northeastern Minnesota's first iron mines. As Duluth was struggling to recover in the late 1870s, George Stuntz had dusted off his Lake Vermilion iron ore samples and showed them to George C. Stone. Stone passed the news of potential iron deposits to Philadelphia's Charlemagne Tower, who sent a doubting geologist to check things out. Stuntz had to practically drag the skeptical scientist up the Vermilion Trail, but his efforts paid off: they found substantial iron deposits. By 1883 a mining company organized by Tower and Stone was ready to start digging.

Tower's group not only opened the Vermilion Iron Range but also built the Duluth & Iron Range Railroad (D&IR) to carry ore to docks to be shipped to steel plants in Pennsylvania. But Tower bypassed Duluth and built the docks at Agate Bay, which then joined with Burlington Bay to form the village of Two Harbors. The railroad began moving ore in 1884 and two years later built a line to carry people and goods between Two Harbors and Duluth. It ran along the shore south to Duluth's eastern border, which thanks to continued bond-debt payments now reached the western border of Endion at Fifteenth Avenue East.

The D&IR line marked the completion of Duluth's second wave of railroad expansion. The NP had finally reached Superior in 1882. Three years later the railroad connected Duluth to the blossoming village of West Superior with the St. Louis River Bridge between Rice's and Conner's Points. Soon thereafter the Chicago, St. Paul, Minneapolis & Omaha Railway built freight and passenger depots along Duluth's waterfront and began offering service to and from the village.

Construction of Duluth's Grand Opera House (1883–89) signaled that the city's economy had turned a corner toward prosperity. *Duluth Public Library*

Duluth Gets an Opera House

In 1883 Roger Munger and Clinton Markell built the Duluth Grand Opera House at 333 West Superior Street. Standing four stories tall, the opulent structure included a mansard roof finished in several shades of purple and crowned with iron cresting. Designed by St. Paul architect George Wirth, it is considered perhaps the most elaborately adorned building to ever grace the Zenith City.

Moreover, it symbolized Duluth's prosperity: after decades of struggle, city founders suddenly had wealth and, with it, leisure time. They spared no expense constructing the town's architectural jewel, and treated its opening-night audience to a performance by Emma Abbot, the nation's premier operatic soprano.

For Munger and Markell and their contemporaries, the opera house also signaled that they were confident Duluth's struggles were behind it. They battled one another for the best of the theater's six private boxes, but Alanzo J. Whiteman, a newcomer from New York, outbid them all. Whiteman came to Duluth to buy timberland on behalf of his father, but wound up representing Duluth in the state legislature, referred to in St. Paul newspapers as the "handsome young senator from Duluth." He was one of many ambitious young men who arrived in the 1880s eager to carve out their own niche in the booming town, men including Guilford Hartley, who would lead the next generation of business and civic power brokers.

More than a performance space, the opera house also housed Gasser's grocery store, business offices, the Ladies Literary Society (precursor to the Duluth Public Library), and later the Duluth Chamber of Commerce. A new, exclusive men's group also took up residence: the Kitchi Gammi Club, organized, its bylaws declared, "for the purpose of social culture" by "individualistic men of prominence, respect, and leadership in the community"—many of whom belonged to the board of trade and the chamber of commerce. The club offered them a place to quietly discuss business and socialize outside of saloons. The building also contained sleeping rooms for well-heeled, single young men who considered themselves above the rabble found in boardinghouses, including Senator Whiteman, who also belonged to the Kitchi Gammi Club.

Wirth designed many Duluth buildings in the early 1880s, mostly grand, brick, Richardsonian Romanesque Revival structures trimmed with sandstone. When Wirth returned to his native Germany in 1886, his Duluth construction superintendent, Oliver Traphagen, hung out his own shingle and became the city's premier architect. Traphagen designed dozens of Romanesque Revival masterworks, both alone and with his partner, Francis Fitzpatrick, until 1896 when he moved to Hawaii—and became its premier architect.

Beginning in the late 1880s, Traphagen and others designed many ornate Victorian mansions between Second and Sixth Avenues East from Second to Fourth Streets, mostly for early residents like Markell and James D. Ray and others who had stuck by Duluth during her struggles and had reaped the rewards of their investments, hard work, and patience. So many of them were connected to Ohio's Ashtabula County that the neighborhood became known as Ashtabula Heights. Today those homes are nearly all gone, replaced by buildings of the expanding Essentia Health campus.

The Village Continues to Swell

A relative newcomer, Vermont lumberman Horace Moore replaced Ensign as mayor in 1885. Moore ran unopposed—and reluctantly, pressed into his nomination by petition. The *Duluth News Tribune* reported that Moore's priorities would be "the introduction of a sewer system, the further improvement of our streets, [and] gas and water."

Hardly glamorous, Moore's goals signaled a growing population that would exceed eighteen thousand during his watch. Some were like Moore, Yankees who took to heart the edict "Go West, young man." Many more were immigrants. They included well-educated Western Europeans—chiefly Protestant English, Scots, and Germans—who like the Yankees came to Duluth with letters of introduction to help establish them professionally. Others were recruited for specific skilled jobs, such as Norwegian and Swedish fishermen, lured to Lake Superior by the A. Booth Company to operate fishing villages along the North Shore.

Meanwhile, Across the Bay . . .

While Duluth first began booming in the late 1860s, Superior remained relatively stagnant, adding just 310 people between 1860 and 1870, which brought the population to 1,122 when Duluth had eclipsed 3,000. A quarter of those Superiorites fled when the Panic of 1873 struck, and by 1880 just 655 people, including some Ojibwe families, lived in Douglas County. Statistician Frank Flower later wrote that in the 1870s, "excitement, even of local character, [had] died out in Superior. Indeed, we may almost say that she was dead, and the grass growing over her grave. The great mystery to outsiders . . . was how the people managed to survive."

Hope for a better future arrived in Superior when the reorganized Northern Pacific Railroad (NP) began expanding eastward in 1881. It ran a line from Carlton, Minnesota—where the NP converged with the St. Paul & Duluth Railroad—into Superior following the path of Newton Avenue (Twenty-Fifth Avenue East today) to the Bay of Superior, where it connected with track that hugged the shoreline beyond the village limits to the western end of Conner's Point. As it did for Duluth, the railroad helped Superior boom. When the NP began service to and from Superior in 1882, the county's population had already climbed to 2,500.

In 1883, encouraged by the railroad construction, General John H. Hammond, Robert Belknap, and others established the Village of West Superior immediately adjacent to Superior at Conner's Point, where it spread south along Superior's western border and west along the St. Louis River. The investors' Land and River Improvement Company began developing the village, laying out streets and constructing commercial buildings.

Hammond, who recognized that the shores along Duluth's side of the river would soon be filled to capacity with industry, began luring new and expanding ventures to Superior, investing in many businesses himself. Soon West Superior hummed with industry of its own—coal docks, grain elevators, and lumber mills, all made possible by Hammond and Belknap.

Superior did not stand idly by and watch. The village also bustled with similar construction projects along the shoreline, including something

West Superior didn't have: flour mills. Many of Superior's enterprises were organized by citizens of both sides of the bay. In 1885 St. Paul "Empire Builder" James J. Hill's Eastern Railway Company of Minnesota, predecessor to the Great Northern Railroad, built tracks to Superior as well.

By 1887 Superior was bigger than it had ever been, boasting 3,353 residents, and West Superior was estimated to house 3,000 more. On March 25, 1889, the Village of Superior (also known as Superior City) and the Village of West Superior joined to become the City of Superior. The following year's census recorded its population at 11,983, an increase of over 1,700 percent in ten years.

While Hammond's name is remembered in Superior thanks to Hammond Avenue, his grandson became much more famous. Music producer and civil-rights activist John Hammond III is known for discovering such talents as Billie Holiday, Aretha Franklin, Leonard Cohen, Bruce Springsteen, and a shaggy-haired Duluth native named Zimmerman who turned himself into Bob Dylan.

But most of Duluth's immigrants were unskilled laborers escaping the problems of their homelands: famine, poverty, and religious or political strife. During the 1880s Duluth saw mostly Protestant Scandinavian immigrants (Norwegian, Swedish, and Danish), along with Catholic Irish, Germans, Austrians, and Canadians, with a few French and Italians mixed in. More than seven hundred Russians had arrived by the decade's end. The first Italians were mostly skilled stonemasons from northern Italy who constructed retaining walls and building foundations throughout the growing metropolis.

Homes soon popped up above Rice's Point and downtown and along the east hillside, increasing the need for a sewer system. Many people kept livestock—chickens, pigs, and perhaps a cow or even a horse if one had the means—and creeks carried waste from both humans and animals into Lake Superior and the St. Louis Bay. By the mid-1880s the "pure mountain stream" that supplied the water for

Booming downtown Duluth and the hillside above it photographed in 1887 looking east from Point of Rocks. *Duluth Public Library*

Duluth's first brewery had essentially become an open sewer, and the brewery closed.

Unable to speak English, and often illiterate and unskilled, most newly arrived immigrants moved into enclaves populated by their compatriots west of Point of Rocks, where they could walk to work at the coal docks, lumber mills, and later flour mills and ore docks along the St. Louis River and Rice's Point. The French hunkered down in an area known as the Glenn at Point of Rocks, and the rest filled in the West End—the portion of the former Rice's Point townsite located above the railroad tracks roughly between Piedmont Avenue West and Thirtieth Avenue West.

One subsection of the West End lay below the tracks and housed poor immigrant families from varied ethnic backgrounds, including Finns, Norwegians, Germans, Swedes, and Poles. The neighborhood sat roughly between Twenty-Sixth and Thirtieth Avenues West from Michigan Street to St. Louis Bay, wedged among the lumber mills.

Turning trees into boards involved stripping logs of bark that came off in "slabs" that workers discarded in the bay. Local residents gathered the slabs, burning them to heat their homes and giving the impoverished neighborhood its name, "Slabtown."

Immigrants kept the population rising, and in 1886 it closed in on 26,000. That November the outer harbor's elevator A burned, taking nearby elevator Q with it. Soon thereafter the St. Paul & Duluth Railroad sold its dock and warehouse at the foot of Third Avenue East. Citizen's Dock had been abandoned years earlier and was stripped to its pilings after the elevators burned, marking the end of Duluth's outer harbor. More grain elevators rose on Rice's Point to replace those lost in the fire.

A City Is Reborn

New Jersey native John Sutphin had been elected mayor earlier in 1886—the reluctant Mr. Moore happily avoiding reelection. Sutphin first arrived in Duluth in 1868 and operated a meatpacking plant between South Lake Avenue and Minnesota Slip—nearby Sutphin Street is named for him. Sutphin would be the last mayor of the Village of Duluth and the first of the reborn City of Duluth.

As Duluth's population swelled between 1881 and 1886, so had the village coffers. Duluth steadily paid off its creditors and was ready to completely eliminate its debt by early 1887. Senator Alanzo J. Whiteman of Duluth introduced a bill to that year's legislative session changing Duluth's status from village to city. It also allowed the community to create a new charter and return to its original 1870 borders, including the Village of Park Point south of the canal, and Endion, whose eastern border was extended to Twenty-Sixth Avenue East. At about this time the northern borders of the former townsites of Endion, Portland, Duluth, and Rice's Point (including the West End) began expanding toward the top of the hillside along what was once the shoreline of glacial Lake Duluth, creating new neighborhoods—including Chester Park—along the way.

Many of Park Point's residents didn't rejoin Duluth willingly—some, in fact, considered the annexation attempt an act of aggression. Duluth's industrialists wanted to develop the bay side of the point as they had the eastern shore of Rice's Point, building a system of wharves and warehouses. They calculated they could create twenty-two linear miles of dock space to serve factories operating all along Minnesota Point. Most Pointers opposed the idea.

So they took the matter to court, calling the annexation unconstitutional. They argued in part that the mouth of the St. Louis River had shifted from the Superior Entry to the Duluth Ship Canal, moving the state line and thereby making Park Point part of Wisconsin. The Minnesota Supreme Court disagreed, settling the case in Duluth's favor in January 1890. Van Brunt suggests Pointers weren't satisfied until a deal was struck addressing the central reason the community left Duluth in the first place: "Finally, being promised a bridge, rather informally and not truly officially perhaps, [the Pointers] surrendered." Park Point rejoined the city, but the canal kept the community an island unto itself, as it would take Duluth fifteen years to make good on its "promise."

Whiteman's bill returning Duluth to city status was signed into law on March 4, 1887. Sutphin was retained as mayor; the city's first official election would be held the following February. On April 11, Judge Stearns delivered the last of the old city bonds, an act historian Dwight Woodbridge described as wiping out "the old disgrace to the city."

Whiteman's own disgrace was about to begin. A few years after he helped reform Duluth, his wife, Julia (daughter of Duluth founder William Nettleton), divorced him. He started gambling heavily and was caught cheating at cards, after which he skipped town and his house mysteriously burned down. He became a notorious forger known as "Jim the Penman," and the nation's newspapers followed his exploits as he tried to avoid Pinkerton detectives, once by diving out the window of a moving train. After his capture in 1904 he spent most of the rest of his life in prison or the poorhouse. The city he helped get back on its feet did much better.

This 1887 bird's-eye perspective map of Duluth made by Henry Wellge shows the Zenith City when it regained its city status and before its borders expanded dramatically between 1890 and 1895. *Library of Congress*

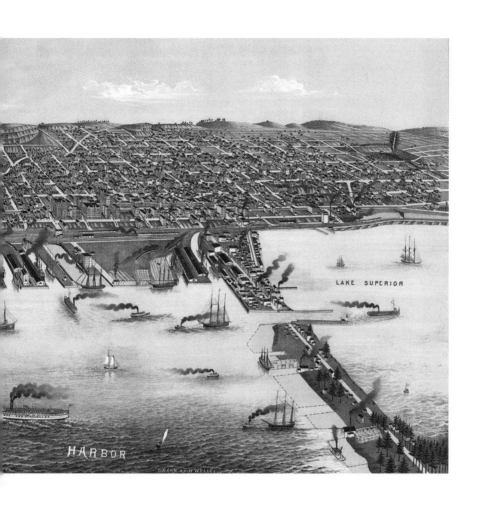

LAKE SUPERIOR

HARBOR

DRAWN BY H WELLGE

CHAPTER 5

Expansion and Prosperity (1888–1910)

The reborn city of Duluth hit the ground running, and its citizens kept Sutphin their mayor through 1890. The new city charter again called for a mayor-council system and doubled mayoral terms to two years. During Sutphin's tenure Duluth improved its streets and sewers and built a city hall, police headquarters, and a new fire station. It also established a paid fire department, school board, library board, and Board of Park Commissioners led by William King Rogers, who envisioned a system of corridor parks along the city's streams, connected by landscaped roadways following the modern lakeshore and the ancient shoreline along the hillside's crest.

The city's prosperity also caused problems. Typhoid epidemics in the 1880s led to the creation of St. Luke's and St. Mary's Hospitals. A strike by street and sewer workers led to a gun battle with police that left three dead and thirty more injured. In January 1889 the Grand Opera House—symbolic of Duluth's success—burned to the ground. Nothing stopped immigrants and fortune seekers from flocking to Duluth, home to 33,000 people in 1890—but the Zenith City was running out of room to house them.

Expanding Borders

In 1891 Duluth annexed several "streetcar suburbs," residential communities north and east of the city made attractive by their accessibility via streetcar lines, including Hunter's Park, Woodland, Kenwood, and

Piedmont Heights. Developers of Duluth Heights built a funicular railway, the Seventh Avenue West Incline, to convey its residents between their homes and downtown.

Duluth's eastward expansion jumped from Endion to Fortieth Avenue East, the western border of Bellville, which in 1871 had been expanded and renamed New London. In 1886 the Lakeside Land Company purchased New London and property east to Seventy-Fifth Avenue East,

The West End Is Not West Duluth

Understanding the local nomenclature is essential to finding one's way in the Zenith City, especially in the neighborhoods west of Mesaba Avenue. In 1870 Duluth's first western border was at Thirtieth Avenue West, the original western boundary of Rice's Point townsite, annexed when Duluth became a city. The portion of the former townsite above the railroad tracks and west of Point of Rocks then became known as the West End.

West Duluth, including the neighborhoods of Bayview Heights, Cody, Denfeld, Fairmount, Irving, and Oneota, lies immediately west of the West End. The elevated rail tracks leading to the ore docks serve as the unofficial border between the West End and West Duluth. Further adding to the confusion is the fact that West Duluth is eight miles northeast of Fond du Lac, the city's westernmost neighborhood.

Besides creating confusion, the West Duluth/West End issue has also caused conflict. For decades residents of the West End resented when their neighborhood was referred to as West Duluth, and those living in West Duluth did not appreciate it when their community was called the West End. Thanks to post-Prohibition liquor-sales redistricting and postwar industrial decline, by the 1960s the West End's commercial center had developed a reputation as rough and uninviting. In the early 1990s local business owners changed the neighborhood's name to Lincoln Park after the existing green space along Miller Creek. Many of those who grew up in the West End still refuse to call it Lincoln Park. Likewise, a portion of West Duluth's commercial district has been renamed Spirit Valley, but to those who grew up west of the ore docks it will always be West Duluth.

The Seventh Avenue West Incline of Duluth's street railway system, photographed here ca. 1900, carried pedestrians and sightseers between downtown Duluth and Duluth Heights from 1890 to 1939. *UMD Martin Library*

creating the communities of Lakeside and Lester Park. Together they formed the Village of Lakeside, incorporated in 1891 as a city. Duluth annexed Lakeside in 1893.

These new neighborhoods rising from the lake east of and including Endion—as well as Hunter's Park—were particularly attractive to wealthy Duluthians eager to distance their families from Duluth's increasingly crowded and dirty downtown. Along the river, another financial panic would spur Duluth's western expansion.

In 1886 the West Duluth Land Company purchased the property surrounding Oneota from Thirtieth Avenue West to Kingsbury Creek and convinced Oneota to join its new Village of West Duluth. The land company aggressively lured metal fabricators to West Duluth, claiming it would become a "new Pittsburgh," a promise that seemed assured when Oneota's Merritt family opened the Mesabi Iron Range seventy miles north of Duluth in 1892. That year the Merritts began building their own railroad and ore dock, both heavily financed by John D. Rockefeller.

Their Duluth, Missabe & Northern Railway (DM&N) made its first Duluth delivery in July 1893—two months after yet another financial panic destabilized the national economy.

The Panic of 1893 didn't crush Duluth as had previous panics, as America still needed what the city provided: grain and flour for bread, lumber for homes, and coal for heat and power. But West Duluth's steel industry struggled, and most metal manufacturers failed. Worse, Rockefeller exploited his agreement with the Merritts, overvaluing his own contribution and calling in loans made to the Merritts when he knew they did not have the cash to pay him back. He took complete control of the Merritts' mining and railroad assets, an act many have described as larceny. By the year's end the village turned to Duluth, hoping to survive by annexation. In January 1894, West Duluth—including today's neighborhoods of Oneota, Irving, Fairmount, Denfeld, and Cody—joined the city.

Cody was named for Cody Street, itself named for William F. "Buffalo Bill" Cody, whose sister Helen married labor journalist Hugh Wetmore and moved to Duluth in 1893. Two years later she opened the Cody Sanatorium, advertised as a "place for delicate women and children to rest and recuperate." After it burned in 1896, Buffalo Bill financed a home on the sanatorium site for the Wetmores, who named it Codyville. (He also paid for their Duluth Press Building at 1915 West Superior Street, which housed Wetmore's newspaper.) Codyville actually sits above the Cody neighborhood in Bayview Heights, which Duluth acquired in 1895. Bayview shares a border with Proctor, originally named Proctorknott for the Kentucky senator who ridiculed Duluth in 1871. Proctor contained the DM&N's rail yard, and Bayview housed many of its employees.

The 1895 annexation also acquired the property between Grassy Point and Fond du Lac along the St. Louis River in the shadow of Spirit Mountain. Immediately west of West Duluth sat Ironton, so named to attract a steel plant. Next came Spirit Lake Park, adjacent to Spirit Lake. Beyond that, New Duluth stretched to Fond du Lac's border at Sargent Creek. In 1890 Atlas Iron & Brass Works relocated from central

Wisconsin to New Duluth and built houses, churches, hotels, and stores for its employees. But the company failed following the panic, dooming New Duluth; meanwhile, Ironton and Spirit Lake Park had remained relatively undeveloped.

Duluth was also determined to take Fond du Lac in the same annexation. Besides its brownstone quarries, the village had become a tourist destination, with excursion steamers carrying Duluthians upriver to its shores for weekend outings on the picnic grounds of Chambers Grove. By 1895 Nekuk Island had become Peterson Island, home to a resort hotel. Fond du Lac's leaders hesitated, worried their community wouldn't receive proper aldermanic representation. It reluctantly joined Duluth on January 1, 1895.

Expanding Population

Duluth's physical expansion was overseen by mayors Marcus Davis and Charles d'Autremont, both Democrats, and Republican Ray Lewis. Annexation increased not only the city's size but, consequently, its population as well. The 1895 census found 59,396 people populating the Zenith City, nearly twice the 1890 estimate.

Duluth's East-West Divide

In 1949 journalist Arthur W. Baum wrote that "the main personality split in Duluth occurs about where an interfering spine of rocks comes down from the hill to Superior Street just a few blocks west of midtown. West of this point of rocks Duluth is politically left, east of it it is politically right." Others might say that to the west lived the poor, to the east, the rich—a sociopolitical divide that took root during the city's industrial boom.

Baum's "point of rocks" is literally called Point of Rocks, a large outcropping centered on Thirteenth Avenue West rising to Third Street. It reached nearly to the bay before street engineers blasted it back. Duluth's unskilled immigrants found jobs in the factories, mills, docks, and warehouses downtown and along the waterfront from Minnesota to Grassy Points, settling in nearby neighborhoods to shorten the walk to work.

So while some found housing in central Duluth, the city's working poor primarily lived west of Point of Rocks. Consequently, western Duluth incubated the city's labor union leaders, eventually becoming a stronghold of Minnesota's Democratic Farmer-Labor Party.

Until hydroelectricity arrived in 1905, the steam and electricity driving Duluth's industry came primarily from coal-fired generators that belched out black smoke. In the 1880s the city's wealthy had built themselves grand homes above and immediately east of downtown in tony Ashtabula Heights, but by 1900 central Duluth was smoky, crowded, noisy, and smelly. The affluent began moving east to newer, fashionable neighborhoods such as Hunter's Park; Congdon, Lakeside, and Lester Park along London Road; and the so-called East End beginning at Twenty-First Avenue East. Most were Protestant, voted Republican, and belonged to the Kitchi Gammi Club, the Northland Country Club, and the Duluth Boat Club.

And so Duluth's unique geography, which lent itself to industrial development along the river and residential neighborhoods adjacent to the lake, unintentionally created a literal and figurative divide. In 2007 beloved Duluth newspaper columnist Jim Heffernan, who grew up in the West End in the 1950s, recalled hearing as a child that East Enders "hoarded money and blocked the paths of others seeking to increase their fortunes" and that "what Duluth needs is six good funerals" of unnamed Duluthians living in the East End.

If Baum visited today he would find liberals, conservatives, libertarians, independents, and others scattered on either side of Point of Rocks, many leaning to the left. He would also see that modest, postwar homes now stand among the East End's grand mansions. But while Duluth is no longer divided between poor immigrants and wealthy industrialists, economic disparities remain, as does the fact that Duluth's low-income housing is still focused west of Point of Rocks and above and adjacent to downtown—and that building stock is aging. Today's Duluth mirrors the nation: a minority are wealthy, the majority struggle, and the middle class is shrinking. In 2019 Heffernan said he believed those funerals have all taken place; a few people in western Duluth likely disagree with him.

The immigrant shanties of the Glenn, aka Little Italy, at Duluth's Point of Rocks ca. 1890. *Duluth Public Library*

Most new arrivals were immigrants, including more Scandinavians, Irish, Germans, Austrians, Canadians, and French. They were joined by Belgians, Bohemians, Dutch, Hungarians, Spaniards, Turks, southern Italians, and a few Asians. While many skilled and professional transplants found homes over the hill and east of downtown, families of unskilled laborers continued to settle close to industry.

Finnish immigrants first arrived in Duluth in 1868. During the boom-and-bust 1870s, Minnesota Point from its base to the canal was called No Man's Land. While its western half industrialized, property along St. Croix Avenue (today's Canal Park Drive) east to the lake contained an enclave of shanties and boardinghouses primarily occupied by Finns. By the 1890s the community included a Finnish church and school and a large bathhouse; locals called it Finn Town. Due to the vermin living beneath their outhouses, the Finns called St. Croix Avenue Rottakatu (Rat Street).

Between Finn Town and the canal lived a group of Orthodox, Lithuanian Jews. Russian immigrants in the 1880s included a number of Orthodox Jews who had settled above downtown, building Tifereth Israel Synagogue at Third Avenue East and Fifth Street. The Lithuanian Jews moved to the same area in 1899, worshipping nearby at Adas Israel Synagogue; the area became known as Little Jerusalem. In 1891 German-speaking Jews from Germany, Hungary, and Bohemia established the Temple Emanuel congregation in Endion, where they practiced Reform Judaism.

The French built homes in the Glenn (also known as Skunk Hollow) amidst Point of Rocks. They were joined by southern Italians in the 1890s, after which the area between Tenth and Fourteenth Avenues West became known as Little Italy. On Rice's Point, Swedish-speaking Finns established Swede Town, called the Garfield Avenue district after other groups moved in. In the West End, German, Polish, and French Catholic churches clustered within a few blocks of one another. Still, the neighborhood remained heavily Scandinavian, as Norwegians and Swedes dominated Duluth's landscape. The portion of Little Italy above Third Street housed more Norwegians than Italians.

This dramatic population increase further strained Duluth's infrastructure, as its insufficient water and sewer system continued to create typhoid epidemics. German immigrant, grocer, and Democrat C. Henry "Typhoid" Truelson won the mayor's seat in 1896 by promising Duluthians safe, affordable drinking water. His efforts created the Lakewood Pump House, which essentially ended the epidemics and today still supplies most of the city's drinking water—and earned him the title of the "pure water mayor of the fresh water city." One of his eulogists said that Truelson "first taught the people of Duluth how to take control of their city government and administer it in their own interest."

Increased Infrastructure and Industry

Seven years after Duluth regained its city status, its citizens were served by sixty-five churches, several synagogues, nearly thirty public elementary and secondary schools, dozens of parochial schools, two nursing

The 1892 Duluth High School, aka Old Central; like the Aerial Lift Bridge and Enger Tower, to many Duluthians this landmark symbolizes the entire city. *UMD Martin Library*

schools, and a business college. Public schools included the 1892 Duluth High School, later known as Old Central, a Romanesque Revival masterpiece that symbolized the city's dedication to education. That same year Catholic girls' high school Villa Scholastica began offering classes, and before the century was over construction would begin on the Duluth Normal School, which later became the Duluth State Teachers' College.

Duluth in the 1890s also housed more than one hundred saloons and dozens of brothels, and its options for more respectable entertainment increased as well. Masons built a new opera house alongside their new temple in 1889. Two years later former village president Andreas M. Miller opened the grand Lyceum Theater. Unlike Duluth's opera houses, it had no private boxes; Miller's socialist leanings inspired him to build a theater for everyone.

Many of those who enjoyed the Lyceum had arrived in Duluth at the new Union Depot, opened in 1892 to serve six railroads, or the nearby Omaha Road's passenger station. Immigration increased as industry expanded on both sides of the bay. Shipbuilding came to Superior in 1889 when Duluth's Alexander McDougall moved his American Steel Barge Company from Rice's Point to Howard's Pocket along the western shore of Conner's Point and began building his revolutionary "whaleback" ore carriers. A whaleback had taken on the first load of ore at the DM&N docks, which by 1895 belonged to J. D. Rockefeller—who also owned most of McDougall's company. The DM&N built two more ore docks before the century ended.

Thirty-four lumber mills lined the bay in Duluth and Superior in 1894, employing nearly eight thousand people. Eight flour mills processed grain in Superior, and while Duluth had only one, it was by far the most impressive; the 1888 Duluth Imperial Mill became the largest flour processing plant in the world until Pillsbury's A Mill in Minneapolis surpassed it. And at least a half dozen fisheries fed more than just the local population, as together they provided 78 percent of the nation's herring.

Duluth also began taking full advantage of its port and rail connections, becoming a major wholesale or "jobbing" center. Warehouses popped up along Lake Avenue between the canal and the railroad tracks and along the waterfront centered on Fifth Avenue West. Their owners distributed and sometimes manufactured a variety of goods, but primarily groceries and hardware. The Stone-Ordean-Wells Company evolved from a one-man operation in 1872 to become the region's largest wholesale grocer. Kelley-How-Thomson made and sold tools for miners and lumbermen and competed locally with Marshall-Wells, which grew to become the largest hardware wholesaler in the United States.

Duluth's annexations began paying off as well. Most of the West Duluth and New Duluth steel fabricators closed by the panic reopened by the century's end. Brownstone from Fond du Lac was used to face

Romanesque Revival buildings in Boston, New York City, Philadelphia, Chicago, and other major cities.

Becoming the Twin Ports

As industrial growth increased shipping traffic, the limitations of Duluth's ship canal and the Superior Entry, along with the harbor's shallow depth, prevented bigger ships from carrying larger, more profitable loads. In 1893 the Duluth-Superior Harbor Improvement Committee, led by McDougall, petitioned Congress for funds to make improvements. Three years later the US Congress appropriated $3 million to make the waters between Duluth and Superior what local newspapers called "the most modern [harbor] in America." The project called for deeper channels—the government was working to make every shipping lane on the Great Lakes twenty feet deep to allow for larger vessels—and for both the canal and the entry to be widened and bolstered with concrete piers. The act also declared that "the harbors of Duluth and Superior [are] unified."

Completed in 1902, the project also increased the population, as hundreds of Finns were recruited to perform the manual labor. Still, Duluth had lost ground immediately after the panic, down ten percent to just under 53,000 people in 1900. (Superior, meanwhile, had risen to over 31,000, making it Wisconsin's second-largest city.) That year Republican Trevanion Hugo narrowly ousted Truelson from the mayor's office, winning by just six votes. (When he won his second election by eight votes, he told newspapers he congratulated himself that he had "made two new friends.") A grain elevator engineer originally from Cornwall, England, the popular Hugo oversaw Duluth's final attempt to keep its 1890 promise to Park Point: the construction of a unique bridge over the ship canal.

Hugo's administration also witnessed the formation of United States Steel (USS). After Rockefeller essentially stole the Merritts' holdings, the Mesabi Range had become a battleground, fought over between his Lake Superior Consolidated Mines, Andrew Carnegie's Carnegie Steel, and Henry Oliver's Oliver Mining Company. Their competition

Bridging the Canal

Duluth waited fifteen years to build the bridge spanning the ship canal it had promised Park Point residents in 1890, in part because of the city's grand ambition to industrialize Minnesota Point. Before the bridge, Duluthians had enjoyed the point primarily as a summer retreat, but federal improvements to the bay in the 1890s included provisions for an "immense anchorage basin" along its bay side. As the point's future factories would require railroad service, the canal bridge would have to include lanes for pedestrians, streetcars, and horse-drawn wagons (and later automobiles), and two heavy-gauge rail lines to carry freight trains across the canal and back.

Another issue was that, while the city intended to build the bridge, the federal government owns the canal, and the canal's purpose is to allow the steady flow of commercial marine traffic in and out of the port. Thus, Duluth required the approval of the US Army Corps of Engineers, which oversaw canal operations, and the Lake Carriers Association, which owned the Great Lakes' freighters. Duluth reviewed bridge designs as early as 1890 and even held a contest in 1891 that drew twenty submissions for drawbridges, swing-arm bridges, and a design for what would become the world's first vertical lift bridge. All were rejected because, in the age of steam, the determining powers felt there was too great a chance that mechanical failure would block canal traffic and cost the carriers millions. The city abandoned tunnel plans due to their high cost.

Fortunately, none of the ideas passed muster. The government expanded the canal in the late 1890s, and any standing bridge would have been rendered too short to span the channel, widened to three hundred feet. In 1898 city engineer Thomas McGilvray developed an idea he found in an engineering magazine: an aerial transfer or transporter bridge, also known as a ferry bridge, that French engineer Ferdinand Arnodin had designed for Spain's 1893 Vizcaya Bridge and France's 1899 bridge over the Seine River at Rouen.

Arnodin's design was simple: a suspension bridge sat atop two steel towers built on piers placed along opposite banks of a waterway.

A gondola car was suspended from the top span with cables attached to pulleys that ran along the structure's bottom rail, which was high enough to allow marine traffic to pass beneath it. A submerged chain, which connected to piers along either bank, was looped over a large drum on the gondola car. A streetcar motor turned the drum, which in turn moved the cables, and so the gondola car essentially pulled itself back and forth above the water.

Fearing Arnodin's design would not hold up during Duluth's often-fierce weather, McGilvray—primarily a street engineer—turned to Minneapolis bridge designer Claude Allen Porter ("Cap") Turner, who made some modifications. The top span would be made of stiff-girded steel rather than suspended cables, and solid steel would also connect the gondola car to the top span. Instead of a partially submerged chain, which could potentially interfere with marine traffic, the drum was connected by cable to a "traveling pulley" system of ball-bearing trucks that ran along the span's bottom rail. It took about one minute for the car to cross the canal.

So when Duluth's Aerial Transfer Bridge—painted olive green—began ferrying people and goods in April 1905, it wasn't the first ferry bridge as many have claimed. It was, however, the first such bridge in North America and the only stiff-girded transfer bridge ever built. Moreover, it forever changed Minnesota Point's future, ending plans for its industrialization: such a bridge could carry only one locomotive or freight car at a time, rendering it highly inefficient for industrial use.

Instead, Park Point saw a boom in the construction of residential housing, and Minnesota Point secured its reputation as "Duluth's playground." Use of the point as a summer resort increased, the Duluth Boat Club moved into new facilities at South Tenth Street, the Duluth Yacht Club operated from its boathouse at South Fourteenth Street, and White City Amusement Park entertained crowds at Oatka Beach. The bridge served Duluth for nearly twenty-five years before it was converted into today's Aerial Lift Bridge.

The whaleback *Alexander McDougall* navigates the Duluth Ship Canal after passing beneath the Aerial Transfer Bridge (1904–29); both were Duluth innovations, and the vessel shown was named for the Duluthian who designed the whaleback. *UMD Martin Library*

intensified until J. P. Morgan felt it was disrupting the national economy—particularly his banks. To avoid another panic, Morgan bought out Rockefeller, Carnegie, Oliver, and others to form USS. The giant company took over Iron Range mines as well as the DM&N and D&IR railroads and ore docks. The deal made many men very rich, including Chester Congdon, Oliver Mining's chief legal counsel. Congdon and his wife, Clara, used their increased wealth to build a grand estate, Glensheen, at 3300 London Road.

The Congdons were just one of many wealthy families who built opulent homes from Endion to Lester Park. They included iron, grain, shipping, lumber, and real estate magnates as well as lawyers, physicians, merchants, and other professionals. The area between Twenty-First and Twenty-Eighth Avenues, including Longview above Fourth Street, became known as the East End. The Congdon neighborhood centered on Congdon Park along Tischer Creek, built on land the Congdons donated. Crescent View developed above Superior Street between Tischer Creek and the exclusive Northland Country Club, founded in 1899 by Kitchi Gammi Club members.

By 1905 Duluthians were claiming that their city was home to more millionaires per capita than anywhere else in the United States, a statement no statistical report has ever supported. The "millionaire" concept was then rather new, and Duluth was among at least a half dozen US cities making the same claim to attract industry.

Hugo left the mayor's office in 1904, defeated by Democratic dentist Marcus Cullum. Cullum and his successor, Republican Roland Haven, enjoyed overseeing further growth. The Aerial Transfer Bridge over the canal began operating in 1905, and a year later the Great Northern Power Company completed construction of the Thomson Dam along the St. Louis River dalles, fulfilling Jay Cooke's 1868 vision. The dam brought coal-free electricity to Duluth—as well as a lot of Serbians, recruited for its construction. They settled in New Duluth and built St. George Serbian Orthodox Church.

More good news came in 1907, first when USS announced plans to build a steel plant adjacent to New Duluth. The company didn't need another mill but offered to build one in St. Louis County as a compromise to kill a proposed state bill for a tonnage tax, which would have dramatically increased USS's operational costs in Minnesota. Later that year Cuyler Adams opened the first iron mine west of Duluth on the Cuyuna Iron Range, named for himself and his dog, Una. Its mines first shipped ore in 1911.

The 1907 shipping season saw the Duluth-Superior Harbor surpass the harbor of New York in tonnage, allowing it to claim title as the nation's largest port. While both Duluth and Superior thrived, a few local industries showed signs of decline: northeastern Minnesota was running out of the pine trees that fed Duluth's lumber mills, and the brownstone quarries were nearing exhaustion at the same time that concrete was supplanting sandstone. The quarries closed by 1910, and by 1921 the lumber industry, considering northeastern Minnesota to be "played out," had moved on to the Pacific Northwest. Still, the success of other industries kept the local economy buzzing.

Cullum regained the mayor's office in 1910, the same year Duluth's population surpassed 78,000. The census declared that the Zenith City was home to 2,772 Finns, more than in any other US community (which perhaps gave rise to another Duluth nickname, the Finnish Riviera). Duluth also led Minnesota cities in its population of Belgians, with 141, but not Scandinavians, an honor that fell to Minneapolis. Duluth held 29,633 foreign-born citizens, including 7,281 Swedes, 5,009 Norwegians,

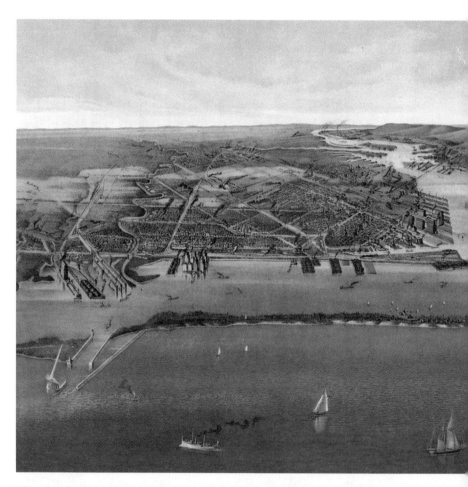

This 1910 bird's-eye perspective map shows Duluth and Superior together as the Twin Ports and illustrates how the river and lake have always connected the two communities. *Duluth Public Library*

4,418 non-French Canadians, 1,423 French Canadians, 2,595 Germans, 1,367 Russians, 1,165 Austrians, 961 English, 648 Italians, 620 Irish, 554 Scots, 405 Danes, 79 Romanians, 76 Hungarians, 69 French, 62 Asian Turks, 57 Greeks, 49 Dutch, 48 Swiss, 31 Welsh, and 363 others from "unspecified countries." Superior's population had risen as well, climbing to more than forty thousand and allowing it to retain its title as Wisconsin's Second City. Together 119,000 people lived at the Head

of the Lakes, and commerce on both sides of the St. Louis River was so intertwined that the two communities essentially acted as one. In 1910 the commercial clubs of both cities decided that the phrase "Head of the Lakes" was both too long and too vague (what lakes?). Along with the *Duluth News Tribune*, the clubs sponsored a contest for a title that would define the two cities as one entity. They selected "The Twin Ports at the Head of the Lakes." Usage quickly shortened it to "the Twin Ports."

CHAPTER 6

Turbulent Times (1911–1929)

By the time Cullum returned to the mayor's office, Duluth's Board of Park Commissioners had made considerable progress on the city's park system. Corridor parks lined the banks of Kingsbury Creek in West Duluth, Miller Creek in the West End, Chester Creek east of downtown, Tischer Creek in the East End, and the Lester River near the city's eastern border. Rogers Boulevard stretched nearly eleven miles along the crest of the hill from Chester Park to Fairmount Park. Mayor Haven had helped organize the Duluth Chapter of the National Playground Association while Cullum himself had secured Duluthians' access to Lake Superior, raising the funds for Lake Shore Park. And then he proposed abolishing the Board of Park Commissioners.

Reorganization

Cullum's plan wasn't directed against parks; it also abolished all other citizen-led commissions that helped the city operate while replacing the system that had thrice elected him mayor. Cullum felt the mayor-council government gave the mayor too much power. Instead, he had become a proponent of government by a city commission, a new, nationally popular system then considered more efficient and better for the laboring class. The city council consisted of five elected commissioners, each in charge of a department: public affairs, public works, public safety, public utilities, and finance. The mayor was the commissioner of public affairs and otherwise played a procedural and ceremonial role, but held no additional powers.

Republican mayoral candidate John A. "Doc" McCuen, the county coroner and popular co-owner of the Duluth White Sox baseball team, opposed the plan. While McCuen defeated Cullum, the incumbent's radical reform passed. But McCuen didn't want to be mayor under the new system, and so he did not seek reelection. Banker William Prince, the former three-time Republican mayor of Bessemer, Michigan, won a hotly contested 1913 election by just six of the 12,323 votes cast.

Prince's fellow city council members included William Hicken, commissioner of public safety, who hit the ground running. Hicken focused on law enforcement—specifically, cleaning up vice, a reflection of similar efforts made throughout the United States during the Progressive Era. He set his sights on Duluth's notorious St. Croix district near the base of Minnesota Point between Finn Town and the jobbing warehouses along Lake Avenue. By the late 1880s St. Croix Avenue's alley housed nearly two dozen brothels. If trade stayed within the district and was practiced only at night, the police left the prostitutes alone—as long as a brothel's madam had paid a monthly fine at the police station. When architect Harold Starin first arrived in 1910, he was told that Duluth's prostitutes "wouldn't give you a tumble outside of their district; they all know better than that."

With the help of police chief Chauncy Troyer, Hicken tried to rid the district of prostitution. The campaign involved paving St. Croix Avenue and changing its name to South First Avenue East. He also went after Marie Le Flohic, also known as Madame Gain, Duluth's most notorious brothel keeper. During her trial, Le Flohic produced an account book listing names of police officers who received payoffs from her totaling $40,000 (over $1 million today) and leading to a grand jury investigation. In what the *Duluth News Tribune* called a "white wash," the police were exonerated while Le Flohic was sent to prison. Despite Hicken's efforts, prostitution flourished in the district until the 1930s, and a handful of prostitutes worked the area as late as the 1970s.

Continued Growth

As its government reorganized, Duluth kept growing. The construction of United States Steel's Minnesota Steel Company plant, which began operating in 1915, created three new communities. Morgan Park, a carefully planned company town named for J. P. Morgan, was originally intended strictly for families of the steel firm's managers, foremen, and skilled laborers—Germans, Scandinavians, and native-born European Americans. It offered one-stop shopping at the Lake View Store, considered the country's first indoor mall, preceding Southdale Center in Edina by fifty-one years. (Technically, Morgan Park did not become a Duluth neighborhood until 1930, when USS transferred ownership to the city.)

South of the plant, Gary—named for USS cofounder Elbert Gary—offered humble accommodations occupied primarily by families of unskilled laborers, many recent Eastern and southern European immigrants and African Americans. Across the river, more unskilled immigrants lived in Oliver, Wisconsin, named for Henry Oliver. Immigrants also found jobs at USS's Universal Portland Cement plant, which used slag from the blast furnaces to make cement.

Duluth's industrial abundance made labor strife common. The Finnish People's College opened in Smithville (formerly Spirit Lake Park) in 1907 and operated until 1941. Established by the Finnish Socialist Federation of the Socialist Party of America, the school made Duluth a hotbed for the Industrial Workers of the World (IWW). By 1911 its students were staging free-speech demonstrations. A 1912 streetcar employees strike resulted in a riot involving some fifteen thousand people. An ore dock workers strike in 1913 was settled with a dime-a-day pay raise, but only if owners didn't have to rehire any Finns. In 1917, one hundred unauthorized national guardsmen marched to the downtown Duluth IWW headquarters and destroyed everything inside.

The working class liked to play. Duluth's laborers and their families took full advantage of the city's ever-expanding parks system and enjoyed several roller-skating rinks, watching the Duluth White Sox, and making weekend excursions to Fond du Lac. They also delighted in vaudeville performances at the Lyceum, Orpheum, Grand (later renamed Lyric), and smaller theaters. The first Edison "talking" picture played at the Orpheum in April 1913, and by the end of the 1920s a dozen movie houses lined downtown Superior Street.

Zenith City Sports

Duluth's history includes many athletic triumphs on the national and international stage. It fielded its first professional baseball team in 1887, playing home games at Recreation Park along the base of Rice's Point. From 1903 to 1916 the Duluth White Sox entertained fans at Athletic Park in the shadow of the ore docks.

Professional baseball returned to Athletic Park in 1936 when the Duluth Dukes first took the field. In 1941 the team moved to the brand-new Duluth Municipal All-Sports Stadium, later renamed Wade Municipal Stadium in honor of team owner-manager Frank Wade, the Twin Ports' "Mr. Baseball." Sadly, the most famous event in the team's history was a 1948 bus accident that killed five players. The team merged with the Superior Blues in 1956 to become the Duluth-Superior Dukes, and over the years it served as a farm club for the Cincinnati Reds, Chicago White Sox, and Detroit Tigers—a dozen former Dukes played on the Tiger's 1968 World Series championship team. The Dukes folded in 1971 and reformed in 1992, playing ten years before moving to Kansas City in 2002. The Duluth Huskies, made up of professional-prospect college players, have called Wade Stadium home since 2003.

Organized by wealthy Scots, the Duluth Curling Club's roots date back to Christmas 1891, and the sport was still chiefly a game for society's elite in 1913 when the club's new facility, then the largest indoor ice rink in the world, opened adjacent to Lake Shore Park. Later Duluthians of all incomes curled, played hockey, and roller-skated on its twelve rinks. In 1976 the Curling Club moved into the Duluth Entertainment and Convention Center's Pioneer Hall. A Duluth team won the men's US national championship in 1964 and 2009 and the women's in 1984, and its junior teams have won seven national championships. The 2018 gold medal–winning US Olympic team featured Duluthians John Landsteiner, Tyler George, and Joe Polo, led by the team's skip, John Shuster, an Iron Ranger living in Superior.

The Duluth Ski Club organized in 1905, and over the years its facilities at Chester Bowl and later in Fond du Lac hosted international ski jumping tournaments that drew thousands of spectators. In 1924 the group built the all-steel jump known as Big Chester, then the tallest ski jump on the planet. The sport remained popular in Duluth for decades, producing Olympians including Gene Kotlarek, Adrian Watt, Greg Swor, and Jim J. Denney. The city demolished Big Chester, its last surviving ski jump, in 2014.

From 1911 to 1923 rowers representing the Duluth Boat Club led by coach James Ten Eyck won twenty national championships when the sport was as popular as professional football is today. In 1920 the Duluth Boat Club's Walter Hoover became the champion of the world, taking the Diamond Challenge Sculls at England's annual Henley Royal Regatta. Hoover received a hero's welcome in New York City and Duluth.

The Zenith City's Kelley-Duluth hardware store sponsored a football team in the nascent National Football League in 1923. Three years later team manager Ole Haugsrud of Superior purchased the squad, renamed it the Duluth Eskimos, and convinced his friend and all-American Stanford running back Ernie Nevers to join. Nevers's national popularity guaranteed ticket sales, so the Eskimos agreed to play all but one game on the road that season, a move league president Joe Carr said "saved the NFL." The team covered seventeen thousand miles, playing twenty-nine games in four months. Along the way, Ernie Nevers's Eskimos, as the press referred to them, became national celebrities—but financial hardship forced Haugsrud to sell the franchise in 1928. Eskimos Nevers, Walt Keisling, and Johnny "Blood" McNally are enshrined in the NFL's Hall of Fame.

Duluth hockey teams won national amateur championships in 1907 and 1917. The Duluth Hornets organized in 1920, going pro in 1924 after moving into the new Duluth Amphitheater and playing until their financial collapse in 1934. Two years later the amateur Duluth Zephyrs moved into the Amphitheater but folded in 1939 after the building's roof collapsed. More recently, college hockey has kept Duluth on the national stage. The University of Minnesota Duluth's hockey teams have won eight NCAA Division I championships, three for the men (in 2011, 2018, and 2019) and five for the women (in 2001, 2002, 2003, 2008, and 2010).

The 1904 Duluth Boat Club facilities along the bayside of Minnesota Point at South Tenth Street. *UMD Martin Library*

The wealthy enjoyed several playgrounds of their own, primarily the Duluth Boat Club. Founded in 1887, it was the largest club of its kind in the United States by 1912, boasting more than 1,200 members. It offered sailing, rowing, and tennis and, after merging with the Duluth Yacht Club in 1907, two grand boathouse facilities along the bay side of Minnesota Point and one at Spirit Lake. Grain broker Julius Barnes, a prominent club member, purchased a "flying boat" in 1913 and named it the *Lark of Duluth*. It was the first airplane to fly beneath the Aerial Transfer Bridge's top span, and later, in Florida, it flew the nation's first scheduled commercial flight. In 1920 Ridgeview Country Club joined Northland, doubling the number of golf links for the affluent.

Fighting, Flu, and Fire

By 1915 news of the war in Europe consumed Duluthians. As fighting escalated, so too did the demand for steel. The USS plant was retooled to make plate steel, and the docks of Duluth, Superior, and Two Harbors worked overtime loading ore from Minnesota's iron ranges. The demand forced Duluth to build its sixth ore dock in 1918—and like each of its predecessors, it was the largest in the world. (Docks five and six still stand.)

Much of that metal would go into ships, many built in the Twin Ports. Barnes and Alexander McDougall formed McDougall-Duluth Shipbuilding Company and started building vessels at Ironton, which they converted into a company town and renamed Riverside. Three outfits built ships in Superior, and together the Twin Ports' facilities produced more than one hundred vessels for the war effort, over half in Riverside. Barnes also served as the president of the US Food Administration's Grain Corporation, which helped feed US troops and their allies in Europe. He gained a national reputation as an astute businessman, and in 1922 he was appointed president of the US Chamber of Commerce.

Attorney Clarence Magney, another Republican, replaced Prince in 1917. Magney had helped establish Jay Cooke State Park and as mayor acquired more parkland than anyone before or since, but mostly he fought fires both literal and figurative: the war was just one of several conflagrations that confronted the city.

Many Duluthians volunteered. They mustered at the new National Guard Armory and paraded along Superior Street to the Union Depot and Omaha Station, where thousands of loved ones provided celebratory send-offs. The *Duluth News Tribune* estimated some five thousand "Duluth sons" had enlisted by Memorial Day 1918; fifty-five of them would not come home alive. Neither would Lydia Whiteside, a surgical nurse who served in a field hospital.

At home the war created other casualties. Anti-German fervor ran rampant. Duluth schools banned German history and language and forced teachers to take a loyalty oath. Finnish immigrant Olli Kinkkonen, a logger and dock worker, had emigrated to America to avoid war. Not registering for the draft made him a "slacker" in the eyes of a local group calling themselves the Knights of Liberty. In September 1918 the Knights abducted Kinkkonen and tarred and feathered him as a warning to others. His body was found hanging from a tree in Lester Park. Authorities never charged his assailants, writing off his death as suicide.

Another conflagration brought more death to Duluth. Following two hot, dry summers, train sparks set off several small fires that combined and erupted on October 12 near Cloquet, twenty miles west of Duluth.

Pushed by strong winds, the fire raced north as fast as sixty-five miles an hour, ravaging communities along the way. The flames mostly swept around the city before dropping into eastern Duluth around 7 PM, destroying the Northland Country Club clubhouse, Homecroft Elementary School, and other buildings. Duluth became a refugee center, with thousands of displaced people finding shelter in the Armory, the St. Louis County Courthouse, and other public buildings. The fire, considered the worst natural disaster in Minnesota history, burned for three days. It left 453 people dead, including 85 in Duluth and the immediately surrounding area; 52,000 more were injured or displaced. The blaze damaged 250,000 acres of land in thirty-eight communities, destroying most of Cloquet and all of Moose Lake, Brookston, and Arnold. Property damage estimates reached $73 million, over $1.2 billion today.

In 1918 the Spanish flu claimed more lives than flames, bombs, and bullets, both at home and abroad. As the war approached its end, the flu epidemic arrived in Duluth. Boardinghouses and residential hotels were pressed into service to house the infirm, and an October city council resolution closed all public buildings—including churches, schools, and theaters—for six weeks. Between October 1918 and January 1919, the flu claimed the lives of 325 Duluthians. Public Safety Commissioner Bernard Silberstein explained to reporters that the city was fortunate, as its per capita death rate sat well below the national average. "If we had the same percentage as in some eastern cities," Silberstein told newspapers, "more than 700 deaths would have resulted."

Bootleggers and Near Beer

More than the weather was dry in 1918. With the Temperance movement marching the nation toward Prohibition, the Twin Ports had opted to ban alcohol early. Superior did so first, closing all saloons on July 1, 1916. When Duluth followed suit exactly one year later, Superior returned to wetness the very same day. The Zenith City's 148 saloons—down from their 1911 peak of 187—closed or became soda fountains, costing three hundred bartenders their jobs. In 1918 Superior dried out again. Each time one of the cities closed its saloons, newspapers reported throngs

Duluth draftees line up to enter service in 1918. *UMD Martin Library*

The ruins of a Duluth residence following the Cloquet–Moose Lake fire of 1918. *MNHS Collections*

An editorial cartoon that appeared in the *Duluth News Tribune* after the city
went dry depicting its namesake, Daniel Greysolon, Sieur du Lhut, apparently
disappointed he has nothing to drink but "Good Old Lake Superior Water."
Zenith City Press

A Postcard of the Hanging

Like any city, Duluth has experienced some ugly moments, but none more horrible than June 15, 1920. Eighteen-year-old Duluthian James Sullivan told police that the previous day an African American circus hand working with the visiting John Robinson Circus held a pistol to his head and forced him to watch as five of his coworkers raped Sullivan's nineteen-year-old girlfriend, Irene Tusken. It was a lie. Physician David Graham examined Tusken and found no signs of sexual assault, but he delayed reporting his findings to authorities. Police rounded up and jailed a group of black circus workers, including Elmer Jackson, Elias Clayton, and Isaac McGhie; all were between nineteen and twenty-one years old.

News of the alleged rape quickly spread through West Duluth, where outraged businessman Louis Dondino began rounding up a mob, setting off a chain reaction throughout the community. That evening a riotous group of several thousand stormed the downtown police headquarters and jail, and within an hour they had broken down its doors. The mob hauled Jackson and Clayton—and later McGhie—a block away to the northeast corner of First Street and Second Avenue East.

Some tried to stop the mob, including Catholic priest William Powers, who climbed a light pole to address the crowd before rioters pulled him down and then used the same post to lynch Jackson, Clayton, and McGhie. The killers then posed for photographs next to their victims before the national guard arrived and dispersed the crowd. Two of the pictures were later sold as postcards. Some of the instigators, including Dondino, were convicted of rioting. No murder charges were ever filed. Circus worker Max Mason was found guilty of raping Tusken and sentenced to thirty years, but was released after serving just four.

Clayton, Jackson, and McGhie were buried in pauper's graves in Duluth's Park Hill Cemetery. The following September the NAACP opened a Duluth branch, and Minnesota passed antilynching legislation in 1923. In 1991 granite headstones were placed at their graves, each bearing the message "Deterred but not defeated," and in 2003 the Clayton Jackson McGhie Memorial Committee installed a memorial to the victims on the street corner opposite of the lynching site. Today Mike Tusken, the great-nephew of Irene Tusken, serves as Duluth's police chief and told the press he considers the lynching "a source of shame and great embarrassment." Tusken joined other Duluthians at the 2018 opening of the National Memorial for Peace and Justice in Montgomery, Alabama.

The 1920 tragedy wasn't the only time someone was hanged in Duluth. In 1918 Finnish immigrant Olli Kinkkonen was found tarred, feathered, and lynched in Lester Park (see page 87). John Waisenen was hanged in 1885 after he and John Norland, both Finnish immigrants, were found guilty of killing a man in Tower, Minnesota. (Norland hanged himself while awaiting execution.) In 1903 African American Charles Henderson confessed to brutally killing his girlfriend, Ida McCormick. He was the last person legally hanged in St. Louis County.

A Duluth police officer stands guard outside a heavily damaged police headquarters and jail the day after a lynch mob stormed the building. *MNHS Collections*

of drunken revelers celebrating "John Barleycorn's last rites" as booze traveled back and forth across the Interstate Bridge between Duluth and Superior. When national Prohibition took effect in January 1920, the Twin Ports' four breweries—Duluth's Fitger's, People's, and Duluth Brewing & Malting and Superior's Northern—had already stopped production. Each began making near beer and nonalcoholic beverages to keep the companies alive and people employed.

A month into Prohibition the *Duluth Herald* boasted that "Duluth today stands as one of the leading cities of the Northwest, with prospects for the future which are unrivaled. Fifty years of steady growth have resulted in wonderful accomplishments for a city industrially, financially, and from a civic standpoint." Nearly all of its 98,917 residents—99.3 percent—were of European descent. Thirty percent were immigrants: 7,455 Swedes, 4,708 Canadians (including 1,093 French-Canadians), 4,283 Norwegians, 3,210 Finns, 1,566 Russians, 1,444 Poles, 1,315 Germans, 878 English, 836 Italians, 731 Jugo-Slavs, 541 Irish, 510 Scotts, 473 Austrians, 417 Danes, 230 Greeks, 131 Czech-Slovakians, 74 Hungarians, 65 Romanians, 54 Dutch, 58 Swiss, and 549 from other countries. Meanwhile, the local Ojibwe population had mostly either moved out of the city or avoided enumeration; just eighteen Duluthians identified themselves as Native Americans. The census counted just 495 African Americans.

Prohibition quickly caused problems. In July federal agents arrested Duluth police chief John Murphy and ten others, including a former US marshal, for smuggling whiskey across the Canadian border. Public Safety Commissioner John Murnian had appointed Murphy chief in 1918, after previous chief Robert McKercher quit and left town ahead of an official probe into his behavior. Murphy had no previous law enforcement experience, and both he and Murnian were already under pressure for their mishandling of a June riot that led to the lynchings of three innocent men, African American circus workers accused of rape.

During Murphy's trial the evidence—ninety bottles of whiskey—disappeared from a vault in Duluth's police headquarters. Murphy then testified that while on a fishing trip he had accidentally stumbled upon

Duluth's Lack of Diversity

While from 1880 to 1920 Duluth was as much a melting pot as any other industrial city on the Great Lakes, today it could hardly be described as ethnically diverse by modern standards. The population of people of color has never been large. Census data reveals that historically the Zenith City has never had more than a few dozen foreign-born Latinx or Asian people living within its borders at any one time. While Duluth once boasted four synagogues, its Jewish population peaked at four thousand in the 1930s. Today approximately 160 households make up the congregation at the Reform Temple Israel while about seventy-five people worshipped at the city's Orthodox Adas Israel, destroyed in a fire in 2019. Those numbers do not include Duluthians who identify as Jewish but are not affiliated with a synagogue.

Duluth's earliest African American residents were also part Ojibwe. In the 1850s, seven of Duluth's eleven African American residents were members of the George Bonga family. Bonga was the son of Pierre Bonga, a free, black fur trader, and his Ojibwe wife. George's brother Stephen, born near the mouth of the St. Louis River in about 1800, lived in Superior. In the 1870s just twenty-two African Americans lived in Duluth, nearly all of them in the Glenn at Point of Rocks or on Rice's Point. That number grew slowly. In the 1880s most of Duluth's African Americans lived in the Central Hillside, establishing St. Mark's African Methodist Church along Fifth Avenue East in 1890, when just 220 people of African descent lived in the Zenith City. In those early decades most worked as porters, waiters, messengers, janitors, and valets. In the 1890s Alexander Miles, a barber turned real estate developer, was considered the richest black man in the region. At the turn of the century, fewer than four hundred African Americans lived in Duluth.

Duluth's African American population grew after the Minnesota Steel plant opened in 1916. That year United States Steel recruited a number of blacks from southern states who agreed to work for less money than European immigrants. Most lived in substandard housing in Gary. Despite the recruitment, Duluth's African American population failed to grow substantially. The 1920 census recorded Duluth's population of "Negroes" at 495, or 0.5 percent. According to historian David Vassar Taylor, race relations became progressively worse in Duluth following World War I, and "restaurants, hotels, and theaters, which had reluctantly served blacks before the war, refused to do so or attempted to establish segregated seating." After the lynchings of three innocent black men in 1920, many of Duluth's established African American families left the city. By 1940, the population had dropped to 314, but it began to grow following World War II. Today about 2,300 African Americans live in Duluth, most in the East and Central Hillsides and the West End, now called Lincoln Park.

Data estimates from 2017 show that 88.9 percent of Duluthians identify as white, 3.4 percent as two or more races, 2.6 percent as African American, 2.3 percent as Hispanic or Latinx, 1.87 percent as Native American, 1.68 percent as Asian, and 0.36 percent as some other race.

bottles of homemade beer and confiscated them. The next day his attorneys produced thirteen sacks of bottled beer to substantiate his testimony. While Murphy and his confederates were exonerated, the chief lost his job; his successor, former federal agent Warren Pugh, promptly fired eighteen patrolmen.

That was enough for Mayor Clarence Magney. After seeing the city through war, disease, fire, two lynchings, and scandals involving two police chiefs in just two years, he left office that fall to become a district court judge. Ever-popular former mayor Trevanion Hugo served out Magney's term, and Duluthians elected Samuel F. Snively mayor in 1921. Like Magney, Snively was a Republican, an attorney, and a lover of parks. Unlike Magney, he remained in office for fifteen years, longer than any other Duluth mayor.

An Ugly Influence

The Twin Ports bolstered their connection in 1927 with the opening of the Arrowhead Bridge between West Duluth and West Superior. As the twenties roared, both cities had continued reaping the benefits of their industrial infrastructures. Grain flowed from elevators on both sides of the river. Coal had reached its apex, with twenty-one docks serving Duluth alone. While commercial fishing had peaked in 1915, more than two hundred fishermen still worked the waters along the North Shore, feeding Duluth's fisheries. The nation's hunger for steel kept the ore docks and metal manufacturers busy, and Duluth's waterfront remained one of the country's busiest jobbing centers.

To top it off, Duluth was a pretty good place not only to live but also to stay alive. In 1925 the Zenith City boasted the nation's lowest death rate in cities of over one hundred thousand people. The *Duluth News Tribune* reported that Dr. L. A. Sukeforth, director of the Duluth Bureau of Health, credited "climate, water, beauty, and comfort, and the greatest of these is climate."

The racial climate wasn't nearly as healthy. Following the 1920 lynchings, most of Duluth's few African Americans fled. Those who stayed did so in the shadow of the Ku Klux Klan. In July 1922 the *Duluth Herald* reported that a Klan chapter had organized in Duluth the previous year and boasted of having recruited 1,500 members. The group said its goal was the "preservation of American ideals and institutions and the maintenance of white supremacy."

Rosters of Duluth Klan members in 1925 and 1926 obtained by Catholic diocese bishop Thomas Welch each list about 250 names. Historian Richard Hudelson describes the group as pro-Norse, anti-immigrant, and anti-Catholic, explaining that much of the Duluth chapter's work "appears to have been focused on urging Catholics from public office and replacing them with KKK members and sympathizers." The listed names were entirely "Anglo, German, and Scandinavian." Members lived from West Duluth to Lester Park, but with "relatively high concentrations in Lakeside and eastern parts of the city."

They included schoolteachers, school board members, a city clerk, a municipal judge, government officials, and a Methodist minister. More than half were war veterans, and several belonged to the police and fire departments, including future fire chief Sievert Hansen. Other prominent names included city commissioners Phillip Phillips and William McCormick and county commissioners Joseph Becks, namesake of Becks Road, and Arthur Cook, who ran the county poor farm. George W. Johnson, then representing Duluth in the Minnesota House of Representatives, later became the city's mayor. Local activity dwindled after 1926, when the chapter's central organizer absconded with its funds.

While the Klan's influence faded, Duluth made moves to modernize. Officials relocated into a new city hall in 1928, as population estimates reached 112,000. The following August Snively presided over a groundbreaking ceremony for the Williamson-Johnson Municipal Airport, predecessor to today's Duluth International Airport. By then workers had begun converting the canal's transfer bridge into a lift bridge. On October 19, 1929, thousands gathered to watch workers raise the bridge's top span forty feet to rest on new towers. Ten days later the stock market crashed.

CHAPTER 7

Depression, War, and One Last Boom (1930–1955)

Two months before the economy collapsed, Duluth's two largest banks, the American Exchange National Bank and the First National Bank of Duluth, merged. For two days fifteen armed guards escorted bank employees carrying $20 million in cash, about $285 million today, from the Exchange across Superior Street to First National. The merger likely saved both banks—in fact, not a single Duluth bank failed during the Great Depression. Other businesses weren't nearly as fortunate.

Battling Depression

The Depression affected every Twin Ports business, and by 1930 one-third of all Duluthians had lost their jobs. The 1930 census shows the city's population at 101,463, so if the 1928 estimate of 112,000 was accurate, roughly 10,500 people—over nine percent—had left Duluth within six months of the crash. (Superior dropped almost 12 percent, to 36,133.) Snively and his fellow commissioners joined with civic groups and business leaders to help end the exodus and take care of those who remained.

One measure created the City Works Administration, which operated much like the federal Works Progress Administration (WPA) but pre-dated Franklin D. Roosevelt's initiative by three years. Early projects put unemployed men to work building a toboggan run and ski jump in Lincoln Park and clearing the land that became Lester Park Golf Course. Another built Miller Memorial Hospital, financed in part by a

One Unique Bridge Becomes Another

By 1927 Duluth's Aerial Transfer Bridge, which began operating in 1905, had become obsolete. With the automobile's increased popularity, there were no longer enough hours in the day to transport every person and vehicle that needed to cross the canal—an issue made worse by the bridge's frequent mechanical malfunctions. Frustrated Park Point residents not only came up with a plan to convert the existing structure into a vertical lift bridge, they also offered to pay one-third of the project's estimated $550,000 cost—over $8 million today.

Lift bridges were nothing new. The first, designed by John Alexander Low Waddell for Duluth's 1891 canal bridge contest, was built in Chicago in 1894 as the South Halsted Street Bridge. By 1930 hundreds had been

Duluth's iconic Aerial Lift Bridge, the city's unofficial symbol. *MNHS Collections*

built, all working on essentially the same principle as a sash window, using counterweights to raise and lower road spans. Towers stand on either side of a waterway. A road deck spans the space between them. The deck and concrete counterweights within the towers are connected by a cable-and-pulley system operated by electric motors. When the counterweights come down, the road span goes up; when the weights go up, the span comes down. Like its transfer bridge, the chief purpose of Duluth's lift bridge is to get out of the way of the canal's commercial shipping traffic. Lift bridges serving the Great Lakes must raise their road spans high enough for the tallest vessels to safely pass beneath, a clearance of 135 feet.

The Kansas City Bridge Company, led by Waddell's former apprentice John Harrington, developed a plan that would retain nearly all of Duluth's transfer bridge. First, the gondola car was removed. Then two new towers were built within the bridge's existing towers, standing forty-one feet taller than their historic counterparts. The top span was then cut free and raised to its new position atop the new towers, after which workers installed mechanical elements—motors, cables, pulleys, chains, counterweights—and a pilothouse. Finally, the road span was connected to the mechanical works. The bridge, originally painted a deep "Essex" green, began service in January 1930.

Like its predecessor, Duluth's Aerial Lift Bridge, painted silver since 1973, became a popular tourist attraction and symbol of the city. Its image appears on all sorts of corporate and organizational logos, including the city's own and that of its police department. While it is not, as many believe, the world's first lift bridge, it is—like its predecessor— unique, as it remains the only lift bridge in the world with a top span, which is absolutely unnecessary for its regular operation. Since about 1915 lines carrying natural gas and later fresh water have crossed to Park Point via the top span; today electricity and communication lines join them. Aerial bridge operators estimated that by the time Duluth celebrated its 150th birthday in March 2020, its road span had been raised and lowered 477,111 times.

trust established by former village president Andreas Miller, who recognized the need for a free, public, secular hospital among Catholic St. Mary's, Protestant St. Luke's, and the city's small, private hospitals.

Construction of the Medical Arts Building, Duluth's art deco masterpiece at 324 West Superior Street, created six hundred jobs in 1932, the Depression's economic low point. By the time the building opened in May 1933, Prohibition was reaching its end and brewers returned to making beer. Of the Twin Ports' four breweries, only Fitger's had remained in business throughout Prohibition, and it never made a profit.

Duluth took full advantage of Roosevelt's relief programs, financing projects from park improvements to downtown storm sewers to keep people employed. Young Duluthians joined the Civilian Conservation Corps, and in 1933 the Civil Works Administration found jobs for 3,345 on projects including a sewage disposal plant and the municipal airport. Author Dora Mary MacDonald reports that by the time the WPA closed in 1943, it had paid nearly $9.5 million in wages for Duluth projects including "installation of sewers and water and gas mains, farm work, streets, viaducts, parks . . . and historical and archeological research surveys."

The Zenith City also finally completed its downtown Civic Center along Fifth Avenue West above First Street, first envisioned in 1909 by renowned architect Daniel Burnham. A cluster of neoclassical municipal buildings designed to boost the population's civic pride, the center is the quintessential example of Burnham's City Beautiful movement. Burnham himself designed the 1910 St. Louis County Court House. An adjacent county jail was added to the plans in 1923, but it had taken until 1929 to get the city hall and federal building standing. In 1935 the city and county—using federal Public Works Administration funds—put the finishing touches on the project, creating an oval driveway and public grounds facing the three originally planned buildings. At its center stands Duluth's Soldiers and Sailors Monument, designed in 1918 by noted Minnesota architect Cass Gilbert to memorialize Duluth's war dead; it features a statue of a knight sculpted by Paul Wayland Bartlett titled *Patriotism Guards the Flag.*

Duluth's Civic Center, 1938. Note the elevated tracks of the Seventh Avenue West Incline in the background. *MNHS Collections*

Snively and His Park Superintendents

Mayor Samuel F. Snively—Duluth's "Grand Old Dad"—was an enthusi-astic parks proponent. An attorney by trade, Snively owned a small farm along Amity Creek above Lester Park. Beginning in 1899 he financed and helped build a road that followed Amity Creek uphill from Superior Street to his farm, crossing the creek on nine wooden bridges along the way. Once complete, he donated the portion below his property, including seven of the bridges, to the city. The road, Snively Boulevard, was later renamed Seven Bridges Road.

When Snively became mayor in 1921, Henry "Gramps" Cleveland was well into his second decade as Duluth's parks superintendent. Dona-tions had helped Cleveland maintain and expand the park system after the Parks Commission's 1912 dissolution. Kindred spirits, Snively and Cleveland pushed for more parks. Although both refused to drive a car, they established "auto-tourist" camps at Indian Point, Brighton Beach, and Chester Park. Property and financial donations by Chester Congdon and his family built the 1926 Lester River Bridge and Congdon Boulevard along Lake Superior, which ran east of London Road's termination at the Lester River to Stoney Point, where it connected with Highway 1, today's Highway 61.

Duluthians of similar spirit also displayed their generosity, in particu-lar Bert Enger, a Norwegian bachelor and furniture salesman from the West End. In 1921 he donated $50,000 for a park above his neighbor-hood, which he insisted include a public golf course. Six years later Nor-wegians led by Gerhard Folgero sailed a replica Viking vessel christened *Leif Erikson* from Norway to Duluth. Enger, on behalf of himself and his deceased business partner, Emil Olsen, purchased the boat and donated it to the city on the condition that it be placed in Lake Shore Park and never removed, and that the city rename the park for Leif Erikson. (Sadly, part of the promise was not kept, as the vessel has stagnated in storage since 2013.)

In 1923 another Bert, West Duluth printer and avid outdoorsman Bert Onsgaard, convinced Duluth to allow him to fence in ten acres in

Fairmount Park for his pet fawn, Billy, and a few other four-legged friends. Within five years he had gathered two hundred animals, many exotic, and the park became home to a municipal zoo that brought decades of joy to Duluth's children and headaches to its politicians. Most of those migraines came from financial issues—concerns that persisted long after the facility became today's independent Lake Superior Zoo.

Cleveland retired in 1925 at age eighty-one, having helped create twenty-seven new parks during his tenure. Snively replaced him with F. Rodney Paine, who had helped create Jay Cooke State Park and served as its first superintendent. Together Snively and Paine developed nearly thirty parks and expanded Rogers Boulevard until it ran from Snively's Seven Bridges Road all the way to Paine's beloved Jay Cooke State Park. When complete, the road was renamed Skyline Parkway.

During the Depression the pair took advantage of every government program offered by the Works Progress Administration and the Civilian Conversation Corps to improve the parks. Duluth's own City Works Administration put seventy-five unemployed men to work clearing land donated by Paine's wealthy friends for a public golf course in Lester Park. Paine also expanded the system by acquiring state and county tax-forfeited properties. Before 1936, Duluth owned just two blocks of beachfront along the lake side of Minnesota Point; thanks to Paine, the entire stretch from the canal to the Superior Entry is open to the public.

Today Duluth's park system consists of about 170 properties and roadways encompassing approximately twelve thousand acres or roughly 25 percent of the entire city. While Snively and his park superintendents were expanding the system, Duluth's population estimates approached 120,000 and showed few signs of slowing down. But the population never officially topped 106,000 and began dwindling in the 1960s. Meanwhile the Zenith City kept creating new parks—and continues to create more. With a tax base of just 86,000 residents, civic administrators find it increasingly difficult to finance the proper maintenance of its public spaces. This leaves the future of Duluth's unique park system—perhaps the most expansive and complex in the nation—a problem in desperate need of a solution.

The 1939 Enger Memorial Tower, built in honor of Bert Enger, who donated much of his fortune to Duluth's remarkable parks system. A portion of Skyline Parkway, completed in 1929, can be seen at right. *UMD Martin Library*

Out with the Old

After fifteen years as mayor, seventy-eight-year-old Samuel Snively left office in 1937, defeated by C. Rudolph "Rudy" Berghult. At thirty-one, Berghult was not just the youngest mayor elected in Duluth but the youngest elected in a US city of over one hundred thousand people. He was also the city's first chief executive born in Duluth, the first to live west of Point of Rocks, and the first Democrat elected in nearly thirty years. Newspapers called him a "student of municipal government and economics." One of Berghult's first actions was replacing parks superintendent F. Rodney Paine and zoo director Bert Onsgaard. Berghult and his parks superintendent, Earl Sherman, oversaw the completion of WPA projects put in motion by Snively and Paine, but following his administration, city officials all but ignored Duluth's parks for decades.

Snively's departure marked the end of an era further symbolized by two 1939 events. In June, Norway's Crown Prince Olav and Princess Märtha visited Duluth to take part in the dedication of Enger Memorial

Tower, built in honor of Norwegian immigrant Bert Enger, who donated much of his fortune to the city's parks. Enger represented the spirit of early Duluthians who shared the fruits of their labor and good fortune by giving back to the city. Just months later the Seventh Avenue West Incline—the last piece of Duluth's street railway system, which had been replaced by buses—was dismantled. It had been built fifty years earlier to serve a booming Duluth and was removed at the point when the city essentially stopped growing.

Duluth's Depression-era efforts helped retain most of its population, which by 1940 had dropped by less than half a percent to 101,065. (Superior, at 35,136, had lost almost three percent.) The city encompassed sixty-seven square miles. More than twenty thousand students attended its three colleges, forty-four public schools, and fourteen parochial schools. Five hospitals, eighty parks, and 105 churches and temples served the city. Eight major railroads brought goods and people to and from Duluth. The city offered jobs with 151 manufacturers, 206 wholesalers, 1,420 retailers, and a dozen banks, while coal, grain, and iron ore continued to flow through the ship canal. Citizens got their news from three radio stations, five weekly newspapers, and three dailies—one published in Finnish.

But while most of Duluth had weathered the Depression, some industry failed. The F. A. Patrick woolen mills closed in 1931 following its founder's death. American Carbolite—which once employed three hundred people making its namesake compound that, when burned, produced acetylene gas—closed in 1943. The fishing industry's annual catch dropped 60 percent and, thanks to invasive species and overharvesting, never recovered as a major employer.

The wholesale food industry also took a hit. The McDougall Terminal, served by its "Poker Fleet" of five refrigerated cargo ships named for the cards in a royal flush, fell into receivership in 1930. The Gowan-Lenning-Brown Company, once the region's premier wholesale grocer, closed in 1933. Four years later, Stone-Ordean-Wells—whose history reached back to 1872—also shut down. The Rust-Parker Company held on until 1947.

The *David R. LeCraw* is launched from the former Barnes-Duluth shipbuilding works at Riverside in 1944, one of 230 ships built in Duluth and Superior during World War II. *MNHS Collections*

Berghult lost the 1941 election to Republican Edward Hatch, a mining chemist from Devonshire, England, who emigrated in 1902. A former mayor of Eveleth, Minnesota, Hatch moved to Duluth as Prohibition began. While he later became chairman of the St. Louis County Republican Party, he first found popularity as the president of the Duluth Dukes, a minor league baseball team. Meanwhile, Berghult joined other Duluth men between twenty-one and thirty-five years old and registered for the draft, as war had erupted in Europe and the nation's entry seemed inevitable.

The War Effort

In some ways, Duluth had entered the fight before the attack on Pearl Harbor, as the city's factories began helping the nation and its allies prepare for war after Hitler's Germany invaded Poland. As elsewhere, the war effort essentially ended the Depression in Duluth. Duluth Brewing & Malting produced industrial alcohol, used to make smokeless gun powder. Refrigerator manufacturer Coolerator built ammunition containers, mess tables, and refrigeration units for the army. Clyde Iron Works' Whirly Cranes—which had helped build the Empire State Building and Golden Gate Bridge—became an essential tool for military engineers. The firm's four hundred employees worked around the clock, as did those at the Minnesota Steel and Interlake Iron plants, producing pig iron and steel. Ore docks in Duluth, Superior, and Two Harbors—practically dormant throughout the Depression—burst back to life as miners returned to work on the Iron Range. It took a lot of steel to fight the war, and two-thirds of it came from northeastern Minnesota mines. Shipbuilding quickly became the biggest industry in the Twin Ports. Six facilities employed more than ten thousand people—including over 3,500 women—to produce an average of ten ships a month while assembling a fleet of 230 vessels.

The Twin Ports also participated in the home front activities familiar to the rest of the nation, from rationing to planting victory gardens to

Duluth: A Bit Off-Center

Outside the Superior Street entrance to the 1926 Hotel Duluth (today's Greysolon Plaza), a compass lies embedded in the sidewalk. Its north-pointing direction arrow sits at a 45-degree angle to the street, not perpendicular as one would expect. That's because, like most of the city's roadways, Superior Street does not follow the cardinal points of the compass but rather the shorelines of Lake Superior and the St. Louis River—another example of the lake's and river's profound influence on the city. In Duluth, for practical applications such as giving directions, east is often northeast, and west is likely southwest.

Duluth's misdirection can cause confusion to newcomers and visitors. In April 2019 a visitor wrote the editor of the *Duluth News Tribune* complaining that the city's street grid made determining directions difficult, facetiously wondering, "What does this teach the children of Duluth?" He added that being out of alignment "doesn't paint Duluth in a very favorable light," and asked, "isn't it time for this error [to] be corrected?"

The writer would have found support in 1856, when those who established Portland townsite platted their community's roadways along a strict north-south/east-west grid, while nearly every other townsite including and east of Rice's Point followed the lake and river. In 1870, when Portland joined those townsites to form the city of Duluth, it was forced to realign its roadways. A half-block remnant of Washington Avenue is all that's left of what has been described as "Portland's platting error." (Endion's roadways also originally followed the cardinal compass points and were realigned by the time it rejoined the city in 1887.)

Today much of the city from its eastern environs to roughly Central Avenue in West Duluth primarily follows a grid plotted along an angle approximately 45 degrees to true north, following the example set when Henry Wheeler platted Oneota in 1856. But as you go further west or above Skyline Parkway into neighborhoods developed after the late 1880s, you will primarily encounter streets running on the cardinal grid.

Duluth's center, as far as its street-numbering system is concerned, is the intersection of Lake Avenue and Superior Street. East of Lake Avenue is east, west of it, west. North of Superior Street is north, south of it, south. Directions in Duluth are given with the unspoken caveat "if the city sat straight on a map." So yes, often when you are heading east, you are actually going northeast; and north, northwest; and west, southwest; and south, southeast. A local's advice? Try not to think about it too much.

Because that sidewalk compass outside Greysolon Plaza serves as a reminder that Duluth is a bit off-center, both literally and figuratively—something most Duluthians don't seem to mind at all. After all, this is the city whose skyway system runs partially underground, where the West End is located in the city's geographic center, and whose annual Christmas City of the North parade is held a week before Thanksgiving. Duluth may be a little bit off-center, but part of what makes Duluth *Duluth* is that here, true north isn't always where you'd expect it to be.

newspaper, rubber, and scrap-metal drives. The Zenith City surpassed its quota for selling war bonds and victory bonds by an average of 151 percent each drive. By 1942 Duluth boasted 2,500 air raid wardens and the Coast Guard had begun a Harbor Patrol—the Twin Ports were considered invaluable to the nation's war effort, and great measures were taken to prevent sabotage. When the city participated in blackout tests designed to "hide" it from Axis bombers, officials even turned off the green beacon atop Enger Tower.

About fourteen thousand Duluth men served in the war, and about six hundred never returned. Private Michael "Mike" Colallilo and Major Henry Courtney each received the Congressional Medal of Honor, Courtney posthumously; former mayor Berghult was awarded a bronze star. Numbers are not available for the likely thousands of local women who joined the Women Accepted for Volunteer Emergency Service (WAVES), the Women's Army Corps (WAC), and the United States Coast Guard Women's Reserve (SPAR) or served as nurses.

Postwar Duluth

By the time the war ended, printer and former Minnesota Steel Plant paymaster George W. Johnson had replaced Hatch as mayor. The Republican, another West Duluthian, had served as the district's congressman from 1925 to 1937, including two years as Speaker of the House. He is also listed on the Duluth Ku Klux Klan's 1926 membership roster. Johnson held the mayor's seat for two terms, and his time in office was prosperous for the city, which was profiled in the *Saturday Evening Post* in 1949. The author, Arthur W. Baum, painted a fun and fascinating portrait of Duluth, including this excerpt:

> The city of Duluth lies at the most westerly point of the largest, unsalted sea in the world, Lake Superior—a fluid deity which the city worships to a man. . . . At its sharp western nose, where it is fed by the St. Louis River, is the very headwater of all the Great Lakes, 603 feet above the ocean. . . .
>
> Some of the oldest known rock on earth rears up on the north, or Minnesota, side of the bay, river and lake. For some unaccountable reason,

Duluth has plastered itself against this rocky bluff with only a spatter of beach and a couple of sandspits for footing. It is consequently a long, skinny city, a sort of rip-saw blade with smooth edge to the water and teeth sticking up into the rocks wherever it finds a grudging crevice. Like the dachshund, Duluth is a city and a half long and a tenth of a city-wide. Twenty-six miles from one end to the other, its average width is only one-tenth its length, yet it covers more area than Boston, St. Louis or Pittsburgh.

Across the river and inner bay behind a nine-mile sandbar there is a perfectly logical place for a city. In fact, one is there—Superior, Wisconsin. That Duluth, rather than develop in comfort on the grassy flats where Superior lies, chose to buck the unlikely cliffs on the north shore is quite in character. Duluth's history is a long series of counterpunches at circumstances and events. When Duluth wins a round, it habitually comes up off the canvas to do it.

Baum's description went on to depict the thriving city Duluth then was. The local economy remained strong. Bolstered by the continued need for iron ore, grain, and coal, and the ongoing success of the city's hardware wholesalers, the Twin Ports remained the largest inland harbor in the world and second in tonnage only to New York Harbor. Servicemen had returned home with the opportunity to go to college on the GI Bill, and in 1947 efforts led by banker Richard Griggs paid off when the Duluth State Teachers' College, previously the Duluth Normal School, became the University of Minnesota Duluth (UMD). The next year Griggs himself purchased former dairy land for a new, 160-acre campus not far from the College of St. Scholastica, which had evolved from Sacred Heart Institute.

The GI Bill also came in handy for building homes, which were in short supply as the city's population increased with the postwar baby boom. Driveways and garages sprung up between homes built before automobiles became affordable. Modern and relatively modest houses were built among East End mansions whose owners could no longer afford to operate grand estates. Neighborhoods, particularly Piedmont Heights, Duluth Heights, Woodland, Lakeside, and Lester Park, pushed beyond their borders. The chamber of commerce declared 1949 the best building year in the city's history. Duluth in 1950 was home to 104,511 people, and East Junior High became East High School to accommodate the increasing size of the student body.

While the world war was over, the Cold War had already begun, and Duluth's potential as a military target remained. In 1948 the municipal airport had become home to a Minnesota Air National Guard fighter-interceptor squadron, and three years later the US Air Force announced it would spend $10 million creating a base for the 515th Air Defense Command. The facility would later include a Semi-Automatic Ground Environment (SAGE) Direction Center, designed to guide twenty-eight Bomarc missiles housed just north of Duluth along the French River. (The SAGE facility and missile base closed in 1966 and the missiles were removed by 1972; while the air force is gone, the Minnesota Air National Guard remains, represented today by the 148th Fighter Wing.)

Television arrived in the Zenith City in 1953, just in time to share the news that the Korean War—which claimed the lives of twenty-five Duluthians—had ended. That year Duluth voters decided they'd had enough of George Johnson so they elected . . . George Johnson. Democrat George D. Johnson had grown up in Morgan Park and found work, as had his immigrant father—and his mayoral predecessor—at the adjacent steel plant. He rose to a management position and served as president of two local unions. Rumors following the election whispered that local DFL officials selected George D. as their candidate because of his name, hoping to confuse voters and perhaps get a more favorable slot on the era's mechanical voting machines.

By the time George D. took office, commission governments were regarded as outdated, inefficient, and prone to political influence. An advisory committee suggested a mayor-council system, with a mayor acting as the executive branch and a city council—made up of nine members, five representing geographic districts and four at large—

as the legislative branch. Johnson later remembered that two of his fellow commissioners "violently opposed" the idea while the other two
had little or no opinion. The mayor admitted to begrudgingly supporting the idea because he felt the low pay commissioners received rendered them vulnerable to corruption. But by backing the new system,
Johnson was essentially throwing himself out of office.

CHAPTER 8

Decline and Adaptation
(1956–1974)

In August 1956 Duluth's Armory hosted the largest funeral in the city's history, that of Albert Woolson, the Civil War's last surviving Union or Confederate soldier, who died at age 109. Earlier that year Duluthians voted nearly two to one to toss out the commission system. Months later they elected a new city council, which included Lucile Roemer, the first woman voted into public office in Duluth. Eugene Lambert, a native of Cloquet and a labor relations specialist, defeated Johnson for the mayor's seat. Lambert, executive secretary of the Duluth Builders Exchange, focused on the government reorganization. With the city struggling financially and its municipal services compromised, he established two goals: coordinate city functions to make the city run more efficiently and, he told local newspapers, "restore confidence of the 'man on the street' in Duluth's municipal government."

Industrial Decline

Two months into his job Lambert told the *Duluth Herald* that his biggest irritation so far was his new mustache. Like nearly every other adult male in the city, Lambert had grown out his facial hair as part of the city's Centennial Celebration of the 1856 founding of the original Duluth townsite. That summer featured pageants and parades as the city blossomed with beards.

Those with fuzzy faces included the few remaining brewers and bottlers of West Duluth's People's Brewing Company. Thanks to the growing national highway system and the advent of refrigerated semi-trailers, several large breweries had gone national, offering their well-advertised brands at prices small-market breweries couldn't match. People's shut down a year later, one of the many large manufacturing plants the city would lose between 1950 and the 1980s. As the population grew with the postwar baby boom, the nation was changing. Larger firms began buying up their smaller competitors, consolidating manufacturing and closing redundant facilities. And every new mile of interstate highway made the Duluth-Superior Harbor less vital.

Duluth's Universal Match Company, established in 1903 as Union Match, could make enough wooden matches in a day to fill two railroad cars, but by 1950 the demand significantly decreased and the company closed. Klearflax, which used flax straw to manufacture linen rugs, employed three hundred people before the war; a larger competitor bought the company in 1953 and shuttered the Duluth facility. Coolerator employed 1,700 workers at two plants after the war, shipping refrigerators as far away as Sweden, but after changing hands both plants closed by 1955. Duluth's only flour mill, Duluth Universal Milling Company, shut down in 1957. Hardware wholesaling began to wane before the war and by 1950 sales had declined significantly. Marshall-Wells and Kelley-How-Thomson merged in 1955 in an attempt to keep both firms afloat, but they sank into liquidation within three years. Bridgeman-Russell, a dairy dating back to 1888, was sold twice before new owners shuttered its massive West Michigan Street facility in 1963. The Interlake Iron Company, the country's largest producer of pig iron in 1955, closed in 1962 after demand for its product dramatically dropped.

There was some good news. In 1950 Jeno Paulucci, Duluth's self-described "incurable entrepreneur," remodeled the Universal Match Company plant to process his Chun King line of Chinese foods. Eight years later he expanded operations, retrofitting Coolerator's New Duluth facility, and by 1960 Chun King sold over half the nation's prepared Chinese food. In 1966 more grain passed through the Twin Ports than in any previous year.

Iron ore shipments had remained high through the early 1950s, in part because of the conflict in Korea—but northeastern Minnesota was running out of high-grade ore. The Vermilion Iron Range closed by 1960, and the Cuyuna held on for roughly another fifteen years. The Mesabi survived because of taconite, a flint-like rock with high silica and magnetite ore content, considered a waste product. University of Minnesota scientists developed the process that made it a valuable resource: the mineral is processed to isolate its iron, which is mixed with limestone and bentonite clay, rolled into pellets, and then subjected to extremely high temperatures that turn magnetite into hematite—ideal for making steel. In 1956 ore docks in the Twin Ports, Two Harbors, and up the shore at Silver Bay's new Reserve Mining facility began loading ore boats with taconite pellets.

Duluth's long-awaited dream of a direct link with the Atlantic Ocean came true on May 4, 1959, when some 3,500 Duluthians lined the Duluth Ship Canal's piers to witness the arrival of the freighter *Ramon de Larrinaga* out of Liverpool, England—the first saltwater vessel to pass through the canal, marking the symbolic completion of the St. Lawrence Seaway. While it had been possible for oceangoing vessels to reach Duluth, the earlier limitations of the Welland Canal connecting Lake Ontario and Lake Erie restricted passage to vessels shorter than 250 feet. Duluth civic and business leaders—particularly Julius Barnes—had lobbied for the larger seaway since the end of World War I. "Duluth yearns so passionately for a St. Lawrence Seaway," noted a *Saturday Evening Post* story in 1949, "that it has been called 'an old maid city looking under its bed every night for an ocean.'"

Improvements made to the canals and locks beginning in 1953 allowed 730-foot-long salties to reach the Great Lakes, making the Duluth-Superior Harbor the world's farthest-inland seaport. Anticipating the increased harbor activity that would certainly follow, legislation in 1955 created the Duluth Seaway Port Authority to improve the city's harbor facilities. Its flagship project was the Arthur M. Clure Public Marine Terminal on Rice's Point, a $10 million, 120-acre cargo facility with its own designated foreign-trade zone, financed with state, county, and city funds.

The *Ramon de Larrinaga* arrives in Duluth on May 4, 1959, symbolically marking the completion of the St. Lawrence Seaway. *Lake Superior Maritime Collection*

Two weeks before the *Ramon de Larrinaga* passed beneath the aerial bridge, Barnes—considered one of the "fathers" of the St. Lawrence Seaway—died in a Duluth Bowery hotel room, nearly penniless after having given away most of his fortune. At his funeral Reverend Robert Dickson said that Barnes's spirit would be "aboard the first vessels that come to Duluth" and that "Mr. Barnes' life and works are a challenge to Duluthians to believe in the great potential of their city and area—to see what he termed the 'unlimited possibilities' to be found here." But the world had changed significantly since 1920, and the increased commerce promised by the seaway never reached its perceived potential.

Turning Toward Tourism

The *Ramon de Larrinaga*'s captain, Joseph Meade, accepted a key to the city from newly elected mayor Clifford Mork. Lambert had chosen to not run for reelection. Mork was a native son and longtime school board member who, with his wife, Evelyn, operated a wholesale grocery business at 605 West First Street. As mayor, the Democrat spearheaded the Gateway Urban Renewal Project—which demolished the Mork Food Supply building—and helped Duluth turn its attention toward tourism. Thanks to the postwar baby boom, in 1960 Mork oversaw a population of 106,884, the largest recorded for Duluth in a national census. But as more babies arrived, more jobs departed—and even more were on their way out. Tourism might help ease the loss of manufacturing jobs.

It wasn't exactly a new idea. In the days before antihistamines, the relatively pollen-free air along Lake Superior's shores made the region

Urban Renewal in the Zenith City

By the 1890s, a section of downtown Duluth adjacent to several railroad passenger stations—roughly along Michigan and Superior Streets between Fourth Avenue West and Mesaba Avenue—impressed visitors and newcomers with the luxurious Spalding Hotel and the grand Lyceum Theater, called by newspapers the "handsomest and costliest building in the Northwest" when it was built in 1889. It also contained a heavy concentration of flophouse hotels and cheap saloons that catered to off-season lumberjacks and other single men of the laboring class who had extra time and a little money, both spent on whiskey. The area became known as Duluth's Bowery after the Manhattan neighborhood notorious for similar social issues.

Prohibition failed to fix the problems, and clearing out the St. Croix district's saloons and brothels in the 1930s increased the Bowery's marginalized population. After World War II, the area became home to pensionless retirees and traumatized young men returned from battle. Many suffered from alcoholism and mental health problems.

In the 1950s urban renewal programs across the nation attempted to eliminate areas perceived to be blighted in order to increase urban business opportunities as populations spread outward into suburbs. Duluth's Gateway Urban Renewal Project targeted the Bowery. The city began purchasing and condemning buildings in and adjacent to the Bowery up to First Street. By 1970, nearly all had fallen.

While the razed buildings included architectural and cultural landmarks like the Lyceum, the Spalding, and the Soo Line Depot, most were insignificant. Others had indeed contributed to the Bowery's problems: a liquor store, more than a dozen residential hotels, and nearly as many taverns—the Classy Lumberjack, the Lamplighter Lounge, Green's Crystal Terrace, and the original Saratoga Bar among them. But their destruction simply displaced the problems, as Bowery inhabitants moved to the West End and eastern downtown along First Street.

In the 1960s and 1970s new buildings rose to replace them, including the Ordean Building, the Duluth Public Library, the Radisson Hotel, low-income apartments Gateway Tower and Lenox Place, and others, including an addition to and modernization of the Duluth News Tribune building. None are considered examples of landmark architecture. Among the few buildings left standing was the 1892 Union Depot. Closed in 1969, the building reopened in 1977 as the St. Louis County Heritage and Arts Center, which houses the Duluth Art Institute, the Duluth Playhouse, Arrowhead Chorale, Matinee Musicale, the Minnesota Ballet, the Lake Superior Railroad Museum, the North Shore Scenic Railway, and the St. Louis County Historical Society.

The initial expansion of Interstate 35 (I-35) through the city stopped at the foot of Mesaba Avenue, the urban renewal project's western border. There the city built Gateway Plaza, including a large, concrete sculpture designed to suggest a ship's billowing sail to greet those entering downtown Duluth from the highway. Two blocks east, Julia and Caroline Marshall and Dorothy Congdon privately financed the Fifth Avenue West Mall between Michigan Street and the Civic Center—a grand driveway to the city's symbolic front yard. There, a fountain was installed in the middle of the Civic Center's public grounds and named in honor of Joseph "Petunia Joe" Priley, a musician and county commissioner who instituted a nationally renowned civic beautification program in Duluth. Further expansion of I-35 in the 1980s allowed drivers to bypass downtown, compromising the entire "gateway" concept.

Pat Murphy's Classy Lumberjack bar within the Park Hotel at 531 West Superior Street, demolished along with most of the rest of Duluth's "Bowery" during the Gateway Urban Renewal Project. *Zenith City Press*

View from Priley Fountain in the center of the Duluth Civic Center atop the Fifth Avenue West Mall on the day it opened in 1971; the Duluth Arena Auditorium (left) and historic 1892 Duluth Depot (right) stand in the background. *UMD Martin Library*

an ideal retreat for hay fever sufferers, and those who could afford it spent summers in Duluth or at resorts along the North Shore. Post-cards promoted Minnesota Point as a "Hay Fever Haven" and in 1900 the city became home to the Hay Fever Club of America. The aerial bridge had attracted curiosity seekers since its 1905 construction as a transfer bridge, and its popularity continued after it became a lift bridge in 1930. Since 1927 the *Leif Erikson*, a replica of a Viking ship, was sec-ond only to the aerial bridge as an attraction. Auto tourism, introduced in the early 1920s, took off after the North Shore's Highway 1 (today's Highway 61) and Skyline Parkway were completed later that decade. But in 1960 Duluth did not identify itself as a tourist town.

With support from business leaders including Paulucci, Mork ap-pointed a committee that eventually developed the Duluth Arena Audi-torium on the site of abandoned industrial facilities between Minnesota Slip and Fifth Avenue West. The $6.1 million project—financed by a city bond, federal funds, and many private donations—opened in 1966 and has since gone through several expansions, evolving into today's Duluth Entertainment and Convention Center.

Mork never saw the project completed; he died of a heart attack in August 1962. Congressman John Blatnik was one of Mork's pallbear-ers. Just a year earlier they had together celebrated the opening of the Duluth-Superior Bridge between Rice's and Conner's Points. The new structure not only replaced the Interstate Bridge but also displaced the residents of the Garfield Avenue district, which was cleared to make room for approach ramps. While the bridge was later renamed for Blat-nik, because of its height most locals called it the High Bridge.

Former mayor George D. Johnson finished out Mork's term and won the 1963 mayoral race. He found the city just as he had left it, facing mounting financial problems. City council president Clifford Johnson even suggested saving money by reducing the city's park system, which by then contained more than 120 green spaces and roadways, to just six parks. He found little support.

Meanwhile the city slowly embraced tourism, offering aerial bridge rides beginning in 1965. For a small fee throughout the summer, the curious could stand inside a chain-link enclosure on the bridge's road span as it was raised and lowered. Bridge operators despised the practice as a distraction and safety hazard, but tourists loved it and the attraction continued for nearly a decade. A successful 1966 fundraising effort purchased lights to show off the bridge at night. Unfortunately, the bridge's deep green paint did not reflect the light.

The state's plans to push Interstate 35 (I-35) through Duluth further shaped the city's landscape, as struggling manufacturers in the highway's path were forced to close. Moreover, the highway expansion signaled the continuing decline of railroads. The Omaha Road stopped Duluth service in 1958; the Milwaukee Road in about 1960. The Duluth, South Shore & Atlantic stopped shipping ore in 1962, and Twin Ports passenger service ended in 1969 when the Soo Line shuttered its depots. The following year the Northern Pacific and Great Northern were absorbed by Burlington Northern. (Amtrak later provided passenger service to Chicago, from 1978 to 1981, and St. Paul, from 1978 to 1985.)

Environmental Awakening

St. Louis County purchasing agent Ben Boo, a Republican, defeated Johnson in the 1966 election. While Boo was mayor the city, like the rest of the country, shifted its attention to environmentalism. A year after the passage of the Water Quality Act in 1965, the National Water Quality Standards Laboratory opened along Lake Superior's shore north of the Lester River. It was one of just two such labs in the nation, and the country's only freshwater laboratory.

The lab played a key role in Minnesota's fight against the Reserve Mining Company, whose facility in Silver Bay discharged forty-seven tons of waste rock into Lake Superior every minute. This both muddied the lake's waters and created an unnatural "delta" that destroyed spawning grounds for herring, further damaging the fishing industry. Further, asbestos-like fibers released in this process eventually made their way into Duluth's drinking water. A decades-long legal battle brought by the brand-new Minnesota Pollution Control Agency (MPCA) ultimately forced Reserve Mining to stop dumping, a landmark decision

Disparaged Duluth

In John Dos Passos's 1930 novel *The 42nd Parallel*, a waitress asks a customer, "So you're from Duluth, are you?" Objecting to her tone, the customer asks, "Well what's the big joke about Duluth?" The waitress replies: "It's no joke, it's a misfortune."

Dos Passos's poke at the Zenith City is one example of the many times popular culture has disparaged Duluth over the years. First attacked by Kentucky congressman J. Proctor Knott in 1871 (see page 39), Duluth—like the state of New Jersey—has long played the role of place-name punch line. The titular character of the popular 1905 Broadway operatic farce *The Duke of Duluth* is a tramp mistaken for royalty. Duluthian Thomas Shastid's 1926 novel of the same title treats the term as an insult, as the narrator explains that a Duke of Duluth is "a man who esteems his own abilities and situation in life pretty highly" despite evidence to the contrary.

Dozens of deprecating references to Duluth have appeared in the satirical magazine *The Onion* and television shows and movies, including *Cheers*, *Curb Your Enthusiasm*, *The Late Show with David Letterman*, *The Goodbye Girl*, *The Philadelphia Story*, and others—even *Travel with Rick Steves* took a cheap shot at the city. In 2006 *Saturday Night Live* lampooned the Zenith City in a skit about a fictional, TV morning show's theme song, "Fly High, Duluth!"

In *Manhattan Murder Mystery*, Woody Allen's character states that "New York is the city that never sleeps! That's why we don't live in Duluth. Plus, I don't even know where Duluth is. Lucky me." *Far North*, set in Duluth and nearby Cloquet, includes Charles Durning's character stating that "No man in his right mind is gonna stay up here in this Christ-less country, except us."

Other references are more innocuous, such as the character Major Duluth in Joseph Heller's novel *Catch 22* (1961) or Gore Vidal's *Duluth* (1983), whose portrayal of the city is so inaccurate that the only thing the real city and its fictional counterpart have in common is their name. Sinclair Lewis's *Babbitt* (1922) is set in the fictional city of Zenith, thought to be a stand-in for Duluth, and his *Kingsblood Royal* (1947) references

Duluth several times, likely because he lived in the Zenith City when he wrote it.

Duluth has been portrayed with much more kindness in countless written works by local and regional authors, and without judgment in television shows. A photo of the Duluth Normal School stood in for the high school attended by the *Mary Tyler Moore Show*'s Mary Richards, and while Minnesotan Louis Anderson's short-lived sitcom *Louie* was set in Duluth, the city was only referenced in transitional footage. More recently Duluth has been the setting of several episodes of television shows including *Fargo*, *Supernatural*, and Duluth native Maria Bamford's hilarious *Lady Dynamite*.

Perhaps the most popular joke about Duluth lampoons the city's Scandinavian flavor:

A man boards a bus and asks the driver, "Does this bus go to Duloot?"

"No," the driver replies. "It goes 'beep-beep.'"

that established a government's right to force industry to clean up its pollution. That battle was led by the MPCA's first commissioner, Grant Merritt, a native Duluthian whose family opened the Mesabi Iron Range in the early 1890s. Today the lab operates under the aegis of the Environmental Protection Agency as the Mid-Continent Ecology Division Laboratory.

While Reserve Mining was polluting Lake Superior, a century of industrial use had caught up with the St. Louis River, which had become so polluted that people had stopped fishing below Fond du Lac. Motel owner Willard Munger, who served western Duluth in the Minnesota House of Representatives from 1955 to his death in 1999, became known as Mr. Environment for the legislation he supported. His efforts included establishing the Energy Task Force to Develop Alternative Energy Resources, which brought in millions of dollars in state and federal funding used to clean up the river.

Citizen demands led to the creation in 1974 of the Western Lake Superior Sanitary District (WLSSD) to address problems in the lower

St. Louis River Basin. A year later the national Clean Water Act provided $100 million to build the WLSSD's wastewater collection and treatment facilities, which today serve Duluth and sixteen other communities in a 530-square-mile region surrounding the city. With the treatment system in operation and most pollution-causing industry gone, the water quality quickly improved. People returned to fishing and playing on the St. Louis by the early 1980s, but toxic materials remain in river sediments and cleanup efforts continue.

The environment received another boost—and jobs another blow—when USS announced in 1971 that it would phase the Minnesota Steel Company plant out of operation. While the plant employed five thousand people at its peak during World War II, by 1970 that number had been cut in half. Meanwhile, its aging steelmaking facilities—and the pollution they produced—became major concerns. In 1971 operation was reduced to one blast furnace, cutting 1,600 jobs. The facility held on for eight more years before closing. Soon thereafter the MPCA pressured USS to arrest the air pollutants emitted by its Atlas Cement facility. Instead USS closed the plant, taking two hundred more jobs.

The MPCA also brought an early end to the Fitger's Brewing Company, whose brewery had been dumping wastewater into Lake Superior since 1881. Concurrently, the Minnesota Highway Department's further extension of I-35 threatened to demolish the brewery. Its 1972 closing marked the end of the city's longest-surviving manufacturer and longest-lived industry, beer brewing, whose roots reached back to 1859.

The following year Chun King left town after Paulucci sold the company for $63 million. He then purchased the former Duluth Terminal facility at the foot of Eighth Avenue West to make Jeno's frozen pizzas. The company's biggest success was the pizza roll, developed for Jeno's by Duluth chef Bea Ojakangas, later the author of several highly acclaimed cookbooks. Jeno's left the building—and Duluth—in 1983, but Paulucci and his wife, Lois, would remain influential in the Zenith City.

During Boo's tenure the city also continued its march toward tourism. A big financial boost came in 1967 when Minnesota introduced state and city sales taxes. Two years later, Duluth first established its

Fitger's Brewing Company's bottling house photographed in the 1970s when it was doomed for demolition to make way for the expansion of I-35 until preservationists successfully argued to save it and several other historic buildings. *Pete Clure Collection*

tourism tax, which has since been increased several times. But its local tax base was beginning to wane. The 1970 census showed Duluth was home to 100,578 citizens, down nearly six percent since 1960. As jobs left town, so had people.

Those who remained had a new place to play following the 1973 effort to create the Spirit Mountain Recreation Area, an alpine ski hill intended to boost winter tourism. While initially hailed as a success, like the zoo it became a political headache and financial burden. The next year the city finished shining up the accidental attraction that had drawn tourists for decades, completing a four-year effort to paint the aerial bridge silver so that its 1968 lighting system actually illuminated the structure.

None of these efforts kept jobs, or people, from leaving town. Then Miller Hill Mall opened in Duluth Heights in 1973, further damaging the already declining downtown commercial center as longtime retailers packed up their goods and headed over the hill for brighter horizons and more convenient parking.

CHAPTER 9

Turning toward the Lake
(1975–1995)

Mayor Boo resigned his post to become the WLSSD's director in 1974, the same year the United States began to pull troops out of Vietnam, where forty Duluthians had died in combat. City council president Bob Beaudin served out Boo's term. Like two of his predecessors, Beaudin was a veteran employee of the Minnesota Steel Company plant. Beaudin's daughter Shannon later explained to newspapers that he entered politics because "there wasn't enough talk about jobs." Beaudin ran unopposed in the 1975 general election. During his tenure Duluth tightened its embrace of tourism as jobs, and people, continued to leave.

Creating Canal Park, Part I

Duluth took strides to revitalize its downtown, both to draw tourists and to compete with the ever-expanding retail landscape of Duluth Heights. The city demolished the historic Lyric Theatre as part of its effort to redevelop the upper 200 block of West Superior Street with the Normandy Inn and Normandy Mall, renamed Holiday Mall when the hotel became a Holiday Inn. The project marked the start of Duluth's skywalk system, which connects downtown buildings along portions of Michigan, Superior, and First Streets. After I-35 pushed through downtown, a new link in the system called the Northwest Passage connected downtown to the Arena Auditorium.

Meanwhile, the need for public restrooms near the aerial bridge had evolved into the revitalization of Minnesota Point between the Lake

The Murders at Glensheen

The Zenith City's most famous home is Glensheen, a grand estate built by mining magnate Chester Congdon and his wife, Clara, at 3300 London Road, completed in 1909. Its Tudor Revival mansion is the work of Clarence Johnston, the state's premier architect at the time Glensheen was built. The interior design, with its mix of several architectural styles, captures an eclectic moment in American architecture, but the house—and indeed the Congdons' contributions to the region's history—is often overshadowed by a single event in the mansion's history.

An intruder entered the mansion on June 27, 1977, and used a satin pillow to smother eighty-three-year-old Elisabeth Congdon, Chester and Clara's last surviving child, after killing the heiress's valiant nurse Velma Pietila with a candlestick holder. The assailant left the house with a basketful of stolen jewelry and Pietila's car. The crime, investigation, and trials that followed received national news coverage; today the crime remains the state's most notorious double killing, called "the murders Minnesota can't forget" by *Minneapolis Star Tribune* reporter Larry Oakes.

Almost immediately police suspected that Marjorie Congdon Caldwell, one of Elisabeth Congdon's adopted daughters, had masterminded the crimes. A police investigation led to the arrest and conviction of Roger Caldwell, Marjorie's second husband. After Caldwell's trial, Marjorie was arrested and stood trial, defended by legendary Minnesota attorney Ron Meshbesher. She was acquitted of the charges, after which Caldwell's lawyers filed for an appeal. Hoping to avoid a costly retrial, the St. Louis county attorney's office made a controversial bargain with Caldwell: release for time served following a confession that officials hoped would implicate Marjorie. Caldwell's confession, however, shed no new light on the murders. He was set free, collapsed into alcoholism, and later killed himself.

Marjorie was twice convicted of arson and served prison sentences in Minnesota in the 1980s and in Arizona from 1992 to 2004. She is also suspected of killing Helen Hagen; her third husband, Wally Hagen (Helen's widower); and Roger Sammis, but due to the lack of physical evidence, no charges were ever filed. Late in 2019, eighty-seven-year-old Marjorie Congdon Caldwell Hagen, also known as Maggie Wallis, was alive and living in Tucson, Arizona.

Glensheen, now owned by the University of Minnesota Duluth, opened as a museum in 1979 and has since become one of the most-visited historic house museums in the Midwest and Duluth's most popular paid tourist attraction.

Avenue Viaduct over the railroad tracks and the ship canal. The oldest portion of developed Duluth, this segment of town had gone through many changes, and was known by many names, since Duluth first became a city. In the chaotic boom-and-bust 1870s it was considered No Man's Land. During the 1880s it was divided among residential Finn Town, the Lake Avenue saloons and flophouse hotels of Uptown, and the brothels of the St. Croix district. One hundred years of industrial effort included a tannery, lumber mills, a shipyard, a slaughterhouse, fisheries, metal fabricators, an appliance manufacturer, a mattress factory, and Halvorson Tree, which made brightly colored, three-foot-tall Christmas trees from the lopped-off tops of spruces.

When the federal government improved the ship canal in the 1890s, it also acquired land on either side of the canal. Along the north pier the government built an office building in the Neoclassical Revival style for the US Army Corps of Engineers, which oversaw the canal's operation. The remaining property became green space dubbed Canal Park. In 1938 the city purchased and demolished the nearby Wieland Flats tenement house, built a parking lot on the site, and also named the lot Canal Park.

By the 1960s, while the aerial bridge attracted nearly half a million visitors a year, the rest of the district had deteriorated. The brothels and most bars had cleared out in the 1930s, and Finn Town's shanties went away in the mid-1950s with the St. Croix Redevelopment Project, part of the federal Urban Renewal Program. Manufacturers closed and warehouses stood empty. A scrap-metal yard filled the space between

Abandoned cars line the lakeshore along what is now considered Canal Park, ca. 1970. *Duluth Public Library*

Morse and Buchanan Streets, and abandoned cars and major appliances lined the lakeshore from the canal to the corner of the lake.

Once tourists had enough of watching big boats pass beneath the bridge, they had little to do other than grab a burger at King Leo's—later the Canal Park Inn—and dodge French fry–seeking seagulls. The lucky ones stumbled across Joe Huie's Café within the Metropole Hotel along the Lake Avenue Viaduct as they were leaving the district. Known for its giant butterfly shrimp (and the note on its front door that read "lost key, we never close"), Huie's didn't offer a fine-dining atmosphere but it was by far the region's most popular Asian restaurant and a favorite of Vice President Walter Mondale. The district's three remaining bars, which catered to locals, did little to make tourists feel comfortable. A Holiday Inn opened in 1963, but the same year the Saratoga Bar—forced out of the Bowery—reopened next door as the Club Saratoga, a strip club. Meanwhile, a handful of prostitutes were rumored to still practice nearby.

In 1971 the federal government's Canal Park received an $82,000 facelift, thanks in part to pizza. Jeno Paulucci had purchased the Gowan-Lenning-Brown Building at 525 South Lake Avenue, renamed it for himself, and made it the headquarters of Jeno's Inc. He then bought an adjacent portion of the park to create more employee parking. The federal government used the proceeds to make the area more hospitable to visitors, expanding public parking, adding additional green spaces, and improving lighting.

Back in 1929 the Corps of Engineers had insisted that the aerial bridge's approach ramps include public bathrooms. By the late 1960s the facilities had become decrepit, forcing their removal. Soon thereafter, desperate tourists began relieving themselves in the park. Plans for a bathroom addition to the Corps of Engineers building showed a structure two stories tall to complement the existing structure. Someone suggested the second floor could house an exhibit or two about Lake Superior's shipping history. After philanthropists Julia and Caroline Marshall—daughters of Marshall-Wells Hardware founder A. M. Marshall—got involved, the project expanded into the 1971 Canal Park Marine Museum, today's Lake Superior Maritime Visitor Center.

In 1976 Paulucci's son, Michael "Mick" Paulucci, and Andy Borg purchased the Sand Bar adjacent to the marine museum, filled it with kitschy antiques from their vast collection, and reopened it as Grandma's Saloon & Grill. Their friends in the North Shore Striders running club organized a marathon from Two Harbors to Duluth that summer, and the restaurant served as its finish line. One hundred sixty runners participated in the first Grandma's Marathon, which soon grew into the city's largest summer event, drawing nearly ten thousand runners from around the world. Paulucci, Borg, and others then began buying nearby property, and over the next twenty years what was once the city's most blighted district evolved into its center of tourism, the Canal Park business district—known to most simply as Canal Park.

"Please Turn Out the Light"

Beaudin lost his 1979 reelection bid, finishing third in Duluth's non-partisan primary behind Boo and city councilor John Fedo, who won the general election. The twenty-nine-year-old Fedo, who operated an automobile refurbishing business, replaced Rudy Berghult as Duluth's youngest mayor.

By the time Fedo took office in 1980 Duluth's population sat at 92,811, a 7.7 percent drop over ten years. Fedo's second term began in 1985, just in time for the completion of the Richard I. Bong Memorial Bridge (named for the World War II flying ace from nearby Poplar, Wisconsin), which replaced the Arrowhead Bridge. Coupled with the Blatnik Bridge, also known as the High Bridge, the new span spawned a bad joke: the best way to get from Duluth to Superior and back again is to go over on the Bong and come back on the High.

Between Fedo's first and second terms the continued loss of industry—and jobs—sparked another joke that few found funny. Duluth's disappearing manufacturers included National Iron, shuttered in 1983 during a mining-industry downturn. Two years later a merger moved

This billboard stood in Duluth for several hours in the early 1980s until someone decided the joke wasn't funny. *John Fedo*

Expanding Interstate 35

The expansion of Interstate 35 through Duluth took thirty years. Plans changed many times, and while the effort advanced the city's urban renewal, portions of it were highly controversial, as Duluth lost not just its outdated industrial complexes but entire neighborhoods as well.

Starting in the 1960s, the city and the state highway department purchased, condemned, and demolished buildings to make way for the highway's first extension, from Thomson Hill to downtown. Its path included nearly the entire lower portion of Oneota, former home to National Iron Works (later Davidson Printing), Duluth Brass Works, and Universal Match (later Chun King). Oneota was also home to about 1,600 people whose houses stood among the factories. Bulldozers and wrecking balls destroyed every structure between Michigan and Oneota Streets.

The creation of Oneota Industrial Park took more than two dozen additional homes in the late 1970s. While unhappy residents worked to derail the project, other residents—pleased to get fair-market value for their unsellable homes—countered their effort, which failed. Still more were taken in 1980 and 1981 for the construction of the Richard I. Bong Memorial Bridge, which also created what was called the Oneota Isolation Pocket, a two-block area containing twenty-five houses bounded by the bridge, Superior Street, railroad tracks, and industrial yards. The last of these homes came down in 1984.

East of the ore docks, highway expansion and urban renewal doomed the Helm Addition, also known as Slabtown, between Thirtieth and Twenty-Fifth Avenues West from Superior Street to the bay. Down went more houses, corner grocers, and factories, including most of Duluth Brewing & Malting, forcing the brewery to close. By the time I-35 pushed through the area in the 1960s, the project had destroyed 232 houses, displacing the families that called them home.

The highway expansion also dramatically altered the waterfront district between Eighth Avenue West and the Minnesota Slip. The grocery- and hardware-distribution warehouses east of the slip eventually all came down, as did facilities for the Northern Pacific and Omaha Road railways.

The most controversial portion of the project eventually pushed the highway through downtown to its northern termination at Twenty-Sixth Avenue East. Original plans called for the highway to run along the lakeshore in front of parks and homes from downtown to the Lester River, essentially cutting off public access to Lake Superior. Public outcry and citizen lawsuits led to dramatic changes to the plans. A series of four tunnels prevented the partial destruction of Leif Erikson Park and the demolition of historic Superior Street buildings between Fifth and Seventh Avenues East including the Pickwick restaurant, Fitger's Brewery complex, and the Hartley Building.

Still, many more buildings were lost, including all those along the lower side of Michigan Street from First Avenue West to Fourth Avenue East. Demolition crews destroyed every building between Fourth and Fifth Avenues East along lower Superior Street and from Fifth to Eighth Avenues East on the street's upper side. They included the 1870 Branch's Hall, the city's first brick building, along with facilities that made up Duluth's so-called Automobile Row—car dealerships, repair shops, auto parts stores, and filling stations.

Thirteen houses and several buildings along the lower side of South Street between Fourteenth and Twenty-Sixth Avenues East also met the wrecking ball. Along London Road, the project demolished the Flamette Motel, a gas station, a liquor store, and the Lemon Drop restaurant. Officials spared the Duluth, Missabe & Iron Range Railway's Endion Passenger Depot, built in 1899 at the foot of Fifteenth Avenue East, by moving it to the Canal Park business district.

The expansion forced Duluth to get creative with undevelopable property adjacent to the highway. Space beneath overpasses in West Duluth and the West End became Keene Creek and Midtowne Parks. East of Lake Avenue the city created Lake Place (recently renamed Gichi-ode' Akiing) on top of a highway tunnel, and three other downtown parks—Gateway Plaza, Jay Cooke Plaza, and Rail Park—were all by-products of the project. The I-35 expansion also inspired the Duluth Lakewalk and provided a major makeover of Leif Erikson Park's Rose Garden.

Aerial view of the construction of Interstate 35 through Duluth, 1986. *B. King, Duluth News Tribune*

Clyde Iron's operations to St. Paul. In 1984 the city's unemployment rate approached 20 percent, and Fedo announced Duluth was one of the nation's ten most distressed cities. Sometime in the early 1980s— the precise date is no longer known—Skoglund Outdoor Advertising raised a billboard along I-35 heading south out of town reading, "Will the last one leaving Duluth please turn out the light?" Outrage swiftly followed, and Skoglund reportedly removed the sign within hours. Despite its short life, the billboard lives in infamy.

Duluth didn't stand idly by. In 1986 more than two hundred jobs arrived when the New Page Paper Mill opened in West Duluth. The previous year Duluth again had invested in efforts to revitalize its downtown, spending $7.5 million to repave ten blocks along Superior and First Streets with bricks. As the bricks went down, the city began discussions to bring a new form of entertainment to downtown, working with the Fond du Lac Band of Lake Superior Chippewa to create a gaming casino in the empty 1929 Sears Building. After extensive lobbying, the federal government authorized an off-reservation facility, a novel idea at the time. When the Fond du Lac Casino opened in 1986, the operating agreement called for dividing its net profits, giving the band 25.5 percent and the city 24.5 percent. The remaining 50 percent went to a gambling commission, which then split the money between the two parties. Initially offering little more than bingo, the casino struggled.

In the meantime, Fedo and others—including Jeno Paulucci and state senator Sam Solon—convinced a state commission to bring a convention center to Duluth, resulting in a $17.2 million expansion that turned the Duluth Arena Auditorium into the Duluth Entertainment and Convention Center (DECC), completed in 1990. (Its latest addition, the 2010 Amzoil Arena, is home to the University of Minnesota Duluth's national champion men's and women's hockey teams.)

Fedo's work on the DECC landed him in legal trouble. In March 1988 he confronted a grand jury indictment listing twenty-three counts including theft, falsifying expense records, and attempting to obstruct the state auditor. The mayor potentially faced fifteen years in prison. The theft charge involved $13,500 that Fedo had solicited from three

Duluth businessmen—Jeno Paulucci, Bill Meierhoff, and Wing Ying Huie—to use in his lobbying efforts. During his 1987 reelection campaign Fedo admitted he had passed the funds to an unnamed Twin Cities businessman in exchange for information about competing proposals; Duluthians voted to retain him.

Fedo told local reporters the indictment was "a political ploy . . . motivated by multimillionaire Jeno Paulucci and [Fedo's] other political adversaries." Prosecutors argued Fedo "played a limited role in lobbying for a convention center he later claimed to have won almost single-handedly." They also presented evidence that, they charged, demonstrated how Fedo falsified his travel records after dining on the city's dime with Lory Cossi, secretary to governor Rudy Perpich. After the election, Fedo divorced his wife, Catherine, married Cossi, and was acquitted on all charges.

Creating Canal Park, Part II

Duluth continued its focus on revitalizing the waterfront and Canal Park. Fedo and city planner Jerry Kimball met with the mayors of other struggling Rust Belt cities in 1988. Kimball told them: "We on the Great Lakes have our own history and color, and we must learn to promote it." Fedo said the challenge confronting Great Lakes cities is that they were designed "to face away from the lakes." He urged his fellow mayors "to turn ourselves around" to face opportunities on "the most magnificent system of lakes and rivers in the world." Reviving Duluth relied on reconnecting with Lake Superior and the St. Louis River.

Kimball oversaw the 1985–92 Downtown Waterfront Project that worked in conjunction with the continued expansion of I-35 to further develop Canal Park. South First Avenue East was renamed Canal Park Drive, Lake Avenue was reconstructed, and the entire district underwent a $9.4 million "streetscape" project. The scrapyard became a parking lot, and the abandoned cars and appliances were replaced by the first segment of the Lakewalk. At the lake's northeast corner workers built Lake Place, a park that disguises a highway tunnel; below it the Lake Place image wall, a 580-foot-long mosaic, celebrates the city's maritime history.

Meanwhile former industrial facilities became home to restaurants and retail shops. Hotels rose along the shore where Finn Town once stood. The Marshall-Wells office building became a multiplex containing restaurants, a hotel, condominiums, and offices. Duluth built the Minnesota Slip Bridge for pedestrians to access the DECC from Canal Park, and the slip itself became home to the *William A. Irvin,* a six-hundred-foot retired ore boat that serves as a floating museum.

Canal Park's renaissance continued beyond 2000. The last of the old industrial buildings that could not be repurposed, Zenith Spring, came down in 2006. Despite hopes that highway expansion would lead to its removal, the Club Saratoga relocated on Canal Park Drive, where it became known for its Saturday-afternoon jazz sessions, which ended in 2019. Today Canal Park is home to four hotels, a dozen restaurants, two craft breweries, a craft distillery, several art galleries, and eighteen retail shops. And one strip club.

A Blizzard and a Benzene Spill

Fedo left office in 1992 after losing to Democrat Gary Doty. The November 1991 mayoral race was overshadowed by the so-called Halloween Blizzard. Snow began falling on the evening of Thursday, October 31, and didn't stop until Monday, November 3—the day before the election—blanketing the Zenith City in nearly thirty-seven inches of snow. Some believed Doty would have won by a wider margin if not for alleged shenanigans by Fedo, who was accused of sending plows to neighborhoods who supported him earlier than they were sent to Doty-friendly districts, keeping Doty supporters away from voting booths.

Doty had grown up just west of downtown and worked in education after graduating UMD. He and his brother Ralph, longtime editor of the weekly *Duluth Budgeteer,* both served in the state legislature in the 1970s. Gary Doty then became a St. Louis County commissioner before deciding to run for mayor after learning Duluth's population had dropped 7.9 percent since 1980, down to 85,493. During the 1991 campaign the city's budget reserve dipped below $1 million and its citizens were becoming much more vocal about their deteriorating streets.

Stormy Weather

Once promoted as "the Air-Conditioned City," Duluth is the coldest major urban center in the contiguous United States. In summer, as local meteorologists like to say, Duluth is "colder by the lake," as Superior's frigid waters help keep average daily temperatures between forty-nine and seventy-six degrees. In winter, the reverse is often true, as the hillside protects portions of the city from icy winds. Winters are notoriously long—a year in Duluth, so goes the joke, is "nine months of winter and three months of poor sledding," and Mark Twain still gets credit for saying "the longest winter I ever spent was a summer in Duluth." While he never said it, the statement about New England attributed to him could apply equally to the Zenith City: "If you don't like the weather, wait five minutes." Duluth has experienced its fair share of storms over the years, most famously the so-called Halloween Blizzard of 1991 and the deluge of 2012 known as the 500-Year Flood (see page 153).

At least two other snow events rival the 1991 storm. A March 1892 blizzard blew down chimneys and created twenty-foot-high snowdrifts; it took an army of shovelers four days to clear the streetcar tracks. A February 1922 storm raged for twenty-four hours, leaving behind two feet of snow. Winds snapped cables on the Aerial Transfer Bridge and whipped snow into drifts thirty feet high, covering homes. A three-day blow in December 1950 dumped twenty-five inches.

Home to dozens of creeks, many that drop several hundred feet in less than a mile, Duluth is prone to flooding. In July 1909 a sudden cloudburst sent mud cascading down the Central Hillside's unpaved avenues, causing $500,000 in damage (over $14 million today) and the death of two young children. Newspapers described how Superior Street was choked with mud and cedar paving blocks, "plowed up as though in a seismic disturbance." The problem has increased with the continued development of Duluth Heights, which once contained a shallow lake that drained via Brewery and Buckingham Creeks. That lake has been replaced with impermeable surfaces—buildings, roads, and parking lots—that dramatically reduce the area's capacity to absorb major rainfalls. Consequently Duluth's creeks, many of which have been diverted underground, are often overwhelmed.

One clogged culvert can lead to a lot of damage, as witnessed in 2012 when a blocked Brewery Creek destroyed much of Seventh Avenue East. The same creek had destroyed Sixth Avenue East in August 1972 after nearly three inches of rain fell on an already saturated Central Hillside in just ninety minutes, turning the avenue into a river roiling with trees, telephone poles, asphalt, mud, and rocks. Another deluge struck a month later, covering downtown streets with rubble. A twelve-year-old boy was swept into a culvert and carried two blocks before he escaped. (A similar scene played out in 2012 when an eight-year-old boy was flushed out of a culvert in Bayview Heights after a harrowing eight-block ride.) Damages totaled nearly $40 million—about $243 million today.

Still, central Duluth has nothing on the Fond du Lac neighborhood. The community's first action in 1856 was to turn a segment of Mission Creek into a canal to prevent flooding, but later—due to a low railroad bridge that trapped debris—the creek spilled over every two or three years from 1870 to 1916. Major floods washed out the neighborhood in 1888, 1897, 1909, 1913, 1914, and 1916. Despite improvements to the canal and bridge, large floods struck in 1941, 1950, 1972, 1979, 1993, and of course 2012.

And while the 1975 sinking of the *Edmund Fitzgerald* made Lake Superior storms famous, in Duluth, no "gale of November" was more tragic than the 1905 *Mataafa* Storm. High winds pounded Lake Superior for two days, wrecking or stranding forty-seven vessels and taking thirty-three lives. The costliest wreck occurred at Duluth's front door. The steamer *Mataafa* was trying to enter the ship canal to find safety in the inner harbor when waves tossed her broadside into the north pierhead; she split in two and settled 150 yards from shore. US Life Savers stood helplessly on shore as high waves made launching lifeboats impossible. Thousands of Duluthians joined them, standing vigil along the shore. After waters calmed the next morning, the Life Savers found fifteen sailors alive, but nine had not survived. The storm led to the construction of Duluth's North Pier Lighthouse and the North Shore's Split Rock Lighthouse.

Neighbors along Seventh Avenue East help one another dig out the day after the 1991 Halloween Blizzard dumped more than three feet of snow on the Zenith City. *B. King*, Duluth News Tribune

Near disaster struck the Twin Ports not long after Doty first took office. In the early hours of June 30, 1992, fourteen Burlington Northern railroad cars derailed eight miles south of downtown Superior. A tanker car erupted and spilled thirty thousand gallons of liquid benzene into the Nemadji River, where it evaporated and was carried off by winds, sending a cloud of toxic gas rolling down the Nemadji and into the Duluth-Superior Harbor. At 8:30 AM Park Point residents were told to leave their homes; less than three hours later, the *Duluth News Tribune* reported, an estimated fifty thousand people "in or near Duluth along Lake Superior's shore had been evacuated." The spill sent dozens to hospitals with burning eyes and lungs, but by 6 PM people in both cities were able to return to their homes.

Despite the blizzard and benzene, during Doty's first few years as mayor the city began to stabilize. Projects that began under Boo, Beaudin, and Fedo came to completion, including the I-35 expansion with the opening of the 1,480-foot-long Leif Erikson Tunnel in October 1992.

Two years later Duluth lost one of its oldest major employers as operation of Diamond Tools, founded in 1907 as Diamond Calk and Horseshoe, moved out of state. But with the help of some strong lobbying by Doty, a new business came to town. Cirrus Design, aviation innovators from Baraboo, Wisconsin, moved to Duluth in 1994. A few years later Cirrus developed a parachute for its SR-20 private aircraft, thanks in part to the efforts of test pilot Scott D. Anderson, a Duluth native who also flew F-16s for the Air National Guard. Anderson, who authored several books, died following an accident while testing the SR-20. Cirrus, now one of the city's largest employers, reports that to date the parachute has saved more than 150 lives.

Meanwhile Robert "Sonny" Peacock, chair of the Fond du Lac Band, wasn't happy about the casino agreement, later telling the *Duluth News Tribune* that band members "found ourselves on the outside, looking in on the business we had built." Since the casino had opened, the federal government had passed the Indian Gaming Regulatory Act, which Peacock viewed as an opportunity to revise the agreement. At the band's request, the National Indian Gaming Commission reviewed the arrangement, ruling it did not comply with the new law.

Negotiations led to a new agreement in 1994: the band would become the casino's sole proprietor, with full responsibility over gambling and a larger share of the profits. In exchange for utility services, Duluth would receive 19 percent of gross revenues from slot machines and video games of chance. For the next fourteen years this averaged out to $6 million a year, which was fed directly to the city's street improvement program. At the time it felt like a win for both sides.

CHAPTER 10

Embracing a New Identity
(1996–2020)

Doty won his third election in 1999, a year before the census reported Duluth's population had increased less than one percent since 1990. Duluth's civic leaders pressed on, continuing to reinvent the city's downtown waterfront while a new generation of creative minds began laying the foundation for a cultural and craft revival that would help Duluth find a new identity.

Bayfront Blooms as Local Talent Blossoms

Thanks to the Marshall sisters' Bayfront Park Development Association, the former warehouse district west of the DECC became a public gathering space, further reconnecting Duluth to the St. Louis River. Echoing Fedo, association spokesperson Donn Larson wrote that it was "no longer right for the waterfront to be our back door." Lake Superior, he said—more than anything else—"attracts people and supports our economy."

At the foot of Fifth Avenue West the association built the Great Lakes Aquarium (GLA), a primarily freshwater aquatic museum. After years of planning and financing, the GLA opened in July 2000, but several setbacks hindered its financial success. The city took control in 2002 and has since experimented with several management strategies.

Meanwhile, the vacant land west of the aquarium had become home to public celebrations. In 1987 it hosted the city's first Bayfront Blues Fest, a modest gathering that grew steadily and remains a summertime

Beyond Bob Dylan

Yes, Bob Dylan was born in Duluth in 1941 to Abe and Beatrice Zimmerman, who lived at 519 North Third Avenue East; five years later they moved to Hibbing, Minnesota. Besides his early childhood, Dylan's connection with Duluth is tenuous. He has played the Zenith City just three times and, in his 1998 Grammy acceptance speech, spoke of watching Buddy Holly perform in 1959 at Duluth's National Guard Armory—and that's enough for some Duluthians to claim Dylan as their own. Duluth holds an annual Bob Dylan festival and portions of several streets have been honorarily renamed Bob Dylan Way. But as elsewhere, Duluthians are divided on Dylan: many consider him a genius and others, while recognizing his talent, simply can't stand his voice.

Beyond Dylan, Duluth has incubated many other performers who became famous after leaving town. That long list contains several other musicians including jazz pianist Sadik Hakim, who performed at Thelonious Monk's funeral, and songwriter Sammy Gallop, who wrote Glen Miller's "Elmer's Tune" and Dinah Shore's "Shoo Fly Pie and Apple Pan Dowdy."

Duluth also raised stage and screen performers, including opera singer Millie Baker, who died on the *Lusitania*, and interpretive dancer Emily Schupp, also known as Lada, who toured with the Russian Symphony Orchestra from 1913 to 1922. Broadway and silent-film star Carol Dempster shared scenes with W. C. Fields, and Marguerite De La Motte's fifty-eight movies included *The Mark of Zorro* and two others with Douglas Fairbanks. Big-screen actors included Ice Capades skating star Lois Dworshak and Dorothy Arnold, most famous as baseball-legend Joe DiMaggio's first wife. Jane Frazee appeared in Abbot and Costello comedies while Peggy Knudsen costarred with Humphrey Bogart in *The Big Sleep* and made many appearances on *Perry Mason* and other television shows. Television actors include Raymond Kark, who played roles on *The Andy Griffith Show*, *Green Acres*, and others, while Ira Cook—also a popular Los Angeles disc jockey—appeared in episodes of *Dragnet*, *Marcus Welby, M.D.*, *McCloud*, and *Ironsides*.

Several former Duluthians played roles behind the scenes, like movie producer and screenwriter Sidney Buchman, who wrote *Mr. Smith Goes to Washington*. Russell Mayberry directed over a dozen programs from the 1960s to the 1980s, from *Bewitched* to *Star Trek: The Next Generation* and including *Kojak*, starring Telly Savalas (who married Duluthian Julie Hovland). Emmy-winning writer, producer, and voice actor Lorenzo Music, also known as Garfield the Cat, created the *Mary Tyler Moore Show*, the *Bob Newhart Show*, and *Rhoda*, on which he voiced Carlton the Doorman. Iconic New York news anchor Roger Grimsby portrayed himself in several fictional movies and TV shows, as did Don LaFontaine, a voice actor called the Voice of God, famous for the movie-trailer introductory phrase "In a world where. . . ." More recently comedian Maria Bamford starred in her own sitcom, *Lady Dynamite*.

Other notable Duluthians include philosopher Irving Copi, whose *Introduction to Logic* is a college textbook staple in the United States. NASA engineer Robert R. Gilruth helped pioneer manned space flight, and Richard Nolte served as ambassador to the United Arab Republic. Author and civil rights leader Ethel Ray Nance got her start as a secretary for W. E. B. Dubois, while adventurer Jack O'Brien—chief surveyor of Admiral Richard Byrd's 1928 expedition to Antarctica—later wrote popular young-adult books about sled dogs.

Not everyone left. Margaret Culkin Banning wrote more than forty books and hundreds of short stories and articles for popular magazines, and author Margaret Ann Hubbard penned dozens of children's books and four mysteries, including *Murder Takes a Veil*. The cover of her 1947 novel *Captain Juniper* features a painting by renowned Duluth artist David Ericson. Today the Zenith City teems with writers, musicians, performers, and artists of all kinds.

staple. The site was christened Bayfront Park in 1989 and began hosting other events. The city improved the park and added a stage in 1999 using a $2 million donation by Lois Paulucci. Today Bayfront hosts festivals throughout the summer, and each holiday season it becomes home to the Bentleyville Tour of Lights.

While Bayfront was blossoming, Duluth began paying more attention to its homegrown talent. Duluth's history includes remarkable local musicians who performed music primarily written by others: Jens Flaaten's Third Regiment Band, his brother Gustav's Duluth Civic Orchestra (today's Duluth-Superior Symphony Orchestra), Frank Mainella's orchestra, Joe Priley's big band, piano virtuoso Elsa Anneke, choirs led by Ann Colby Albright, and many others. When rock and roll took center stage, few local bands played original songs.

In 1993 Alan Sparhawk and Mimi Parker formed Low, known initially for its sparse, quiet sound. By the decade's end the group enjoyed an international following and has since released over a dozen critically acclaimed albums. In the late 1990s Scott "Starfire" Lunt launched Random Radio, a pirate station featuring original local music. His thirtieth birthday party inspired the Homegrown Music Festival, which began in 1999 with ten acts playing over two nights at the historic Nor-Shor Theatre. Between 1995 and 2004 the theater became the epicenter

Alan Sparhawk and Mimi Parker of the band Low perform at the Sacred Heart Music Center as part of Duluth's Homegrown Music Festival. *C. Austin*, Duluth News Tribune

Duluth Loses Its Voice

The heavy fog that often blankets Duluth has long hampered marine navigation. The 1858 Minnesota Point Light's first keeper, Reuben Barrett, used a logging-camp dinner horn for his foghorn. Locals called the noise Barrett's Cow.

Engineers first installed an automated fog bell within the Duluth ship canal's original South Pier Light in 1880. Woefully inadequate, it was replaced in 1885 with a steam-powered fog whistle. During a foggy 1895 the whistle screamed intermittently for over one thousand hours while burning forty-five tons of coal. The sound not only warned mariners; it also bounced off Duluth's rocky hillside, creating an unbearable cacophony. Parabolic reflectors were installed to redirect the noise.

An electric, twin Type F diaphone replaced the steam whistle in 1923. Its deep "Bee-Oh" tone could be heard twenty miles away. Duluthians immediately complained—the noise rattled windows, disrupted conversations, and woke sleepers across the East Hillside. But some loved it.

In 1968 a quieter, single-tone horn took over. While some rejoiced, others hated the new "peanut whistle" and felt Duluth had lost part of its very identity. The nonprofit ReTurn Our Old Tone (TOOT) organized to bring the old signal back. It purchased and renovated another antique diaphone to replace the original. The city obtained a Coast Guard permit to operate and maintain the horn, which TOOT leased with the help of a $5,000 annual stipend from the city.

The replacement horn tooted for the first time in June 1995—much to the dismay of many. That night Duluthians barraged Mayor Gary Doty's home phone with complaints, and he ordered TOOT to shut down the horn for the night. The public remained relatively silent on the issue until 2002, when citizens began besieging city councilors with letters both for and against the horn. Despite comprises that led to the horn's limited operation, citizen complaints, TOOT's mismanagement, and disagreements among the three parties kept the debate alive for the next three years.

The issue came to a head in 2005 when the Coast Guard asked the city to stop using the old horn as it interfered with fog-detection equipment and confused mariners. The city hoped to keep it, blasting it once a day and on special occasions, but the signal's power cable had already been removed and all agreed the replacement cost was impractical. TOOT dismantled the horn on September 26, 2006, an action both praised and condemned. The "peanut whistle" still blows during foggy conditions for smaller craft not outfitted with radar and GPS navigation.

of Duluth's growing original-music scene, particularly when it was under the stewardship of Rick Boo. Eventually more Duluth acts went national, including Trampled by Turtles, Charlie Parr, and Gaelynn Lee. Local politicians began referencing the city's "cool factor" while Homegrown kept growing; in 2019 the weeklong event featured nearly two hundred acts in dozens of venues in the Twin Ports.

As Homegrown grew, Duluthians elected native Herb Bergson mayor to replace Doty after he decided against running for a fourth term. Despite his experience as a Duluth city councilor and twice serving as mayor of Superior, Bergson struggled. His critics claimed he wasn't prepared to manage a city nearly three times Superior's size. His 2005 arrest for drunken driving didn't help.

Despite public setbacks, Bergson found some success. In 2005 Northwest Airlines had abandoned its Airbus maintenance facility in Duluth—constructed as part of a state bailout package intended to create jobs in Duluth—which left taxpayers responsible for $35.9 million in bonds. The city brokered a deal to avoid the debt and took possession of the maintenance facility. The late St. Louis County commissioner Steve O'Neil, known for his tireless work helping the hungry and homeless, credited Bergson for his commitment to citizens of low and moderate income, particularly for initiating the first city plan to end homelessness in Minnesota. Bergson was also the first mayor to sign a proclamation celebrating the Duluth-Superior Pride Festival, a gesture Doty refused to make.

While Bergson was mayor, Duluth's school board voted to embark on a $315 million initiative to improve and replace aging buildings, an undertaking known as the Long-Range Facilities Plan, also called the Red Plan. Completed in 2016, the effort generated vibrant public discussions and heated debates during Duluth School Board meetings, some described as "out of control" by local newspapers. One board member who opposed the plan sued the district three times, once because of a board vote in favor of removing him for assaulting the superintendent and board chairman. While the project brought much-needed improvements to an aging infrastructure, projections that it would pay for itself through reduced heating costs and sales of former schools did not pan out. Due to the plan's costs and a decline in state per-student funding, the district struggles to improve student-teacher ratios, keep up with education technology, and provide equitable learning opportunities across schools in its economically divided eastern and western neighborhoods. While Duluthians strongly support their schools—passing levy referenda in 2013 and 2018—concerns about the district's management and budget remain as a legacy of the Red Plan.

Recession and the Flood

Don Ness emerged atop a crowded field of candidates eager to replace Bergson in 2007. Born on the hillside, Ness developed an early interest in politics and served as UMD's student body president. In 1997 he became Congressman Jim Oberstar's campaign manager and took a seat on the Duluth City Council. As mayor, his ambitions were hampered by budget issues, including a deficit approaching $5 million, in the midst of the Great Recession.

Ness and city administrator David Montgomery took on an issue their predecessors had mostly ignored: Duluth's retiree health care program, which guaranteed lifetime coverage to retirees, threatened to bankrupt the city. Bergson's team had made some progress by negotiating a new plan for active employees, but the problem remained unresolved. Ness and Montgomery moved most retirees to Bergson's plan for active employees and others to Medicare, and within five years Duluth's liability dropped by $209 million.

Unfortunately, Duluth's relationship with the Fond du Lac Band soured after Ness took office. In August 2009 chair Karen Diver announced that the band would stop sharing casino revenue as she believed the 1994 casino agreement was entered into "under erroneous understandings that the city's consent was necessary to the creation of reservation land within the city." The city responded with a federal lawsuit. Diver then asked the National Indian Gaming Commission to again review the contract. In 2011 the commission found the 1994 agreement also violated the Indian Gaming Regulatory Act and ordered the band to not resume payments. Duluth essentially lost its street repair fund; unable to appeal the decision, the city pursued the issue through federal lawsuits.

Ness's team also attempted to navigate the recession with unpopular austerity moves, including reduced library hours and deferred park maintenance. Senior city employees were laid off or offered early retirement. The administration also proposed demolishing 40 percent of the city's recreation centers, all located west of Mesaba Avenue. Public outrage put an end to much of the plan. And then came the flood.

A sinkhole caused by the 2012 flood at the intersection of Skyline Parkway and Ninth Avenue East swallowed a Toyota visiting from Washington state. *B. King,* Duluth News Tribune

In the late afternoon of June 19, 2012, rain began to fall, and by 7:15 PM much of Duluth sat under a torrential downpour. By 8:30 its hillside avenues had become rivers. More than seven inches had fallen by the next morning. Brewery Creek, overflowing its clogged culverts, destroyed much of Seventh Avenue East below Skyline Parkway, and manhole covers blew out from Gary to Lakeside. Kingsbury Creek flooded the zoo, drowning most of its barnyard animals. In Fond du Lac, 250 people evacuated their homes, many of which were rendered uninhabitable. Damage estimates exceeded $47 million.

An Outdoor Destination

Once the clouds cleared, state and federal disaster relief funds helped the city repair damage, upgrade its stormwater system, and restore fish habitats along the St. Louis River. The flood recovery also gave the Ness administration a new perspective on the city's western half and its relationship with the river. While the generation that turned Duluth toward the lake had benefactors to help finance its projects, Ness and his contemporaries had fewer financial resources to draw upon—but they had plans intended to both celebrate Duluth's unique qualities and attract young professionals.

One was to embrace Duluth's growing reputation as a mecca for outdoor sports enthusiasts. The city had long offered alpine and Nordic skiing, and in 1998 *Golf Digest* named it the "best city in America for public golf." Ongoing river cleanup brought back anglers and attracted kayakers. The Superior Hiking Trail was extended through the city and the Cyclists of Gitchee Gumee Shores helped the city create the Duluth Traverse mountain bike trail. In 2014 *Outside* magazine named Duluth "Best Town Ever"; three years later the *Minneapolis Star Tribune* called the city "the outdoor capital of the Midwest."

In 2014 Ness also announced his St. Louis River Corridor Initiative, an $18 million plan to invest in public parks and trails along the river. Plans included improvements to dozens of parks and a new chalet for Spirit Mountain. Much of the initiative has yet to be implemented, due in part to a lack of financial resources and also some public backlash.

Many Duluthians felt that aspects of the initiative and other issues concerning the parks had been forced upon them by city officials, including plans for reducing the Lake Superior Zoo's footprint, removing the railbed of the historic Lake Superior & Mississippi Railroad, and selling portions of Duluth's public golf courses to housing and retail developers.

The Craft Movement

Much of Duluth's musical revelry and outdoor adventure was fueled by carbs from beer brewed with Lake Superior water. In 1994 the Lake Superior Brewing Company began brewing small, six-barrel batches on Sundays, becoming Minnesota's first commercial microbrewery. Fitger's Brewhouse first served beer brewed on-site in 1997, establishing itself as the state's first brewpub. Local brewers soon learned what their predecessors had discovered in 1869: Lake Superior water, so soft it requires no pretreatment, makes wonderful beer. Twelve years after Fitger's Brewhouse began brewing, Duluth's craft beer industry had exploded. Five

The principals of Ursa Minor Brewing (left to right): Andrew Scrignoli and brothers Ben and Mark Hugus. Ursa Minor opened in 2018, the newest of eleven breweries in Duluth and Superior making beer with Lake Superior water. *S. Kuchera*, Duluth News Tribune

commercial brewing operations opened between 2011 and 2013, prompting Ness to declare Duluth the "Craft Beer Capital of Minnesota." In 2019 eleven Twin Ports breweries made beer with Lake Superior water.

Beer and other craft industries have helped revitalize Duluth's West End, rebranded by local business leaders in the 1990s as Lincoln Park. The neighborhood had deteriorated during Duluth's industrial demise, earning a reputation as a blighted, dangerous place. The landscape began changing in 2005 when Tom and Jaima Hanson turned a failing Embers restaurant into the popular Duluth Grill. A few years later Alessandro Giuliani turned portions of the former Clyde Iron complex into a restaurant and events venue.

In 2013 Bent Paddle Brewing Company began making beer in Lincoln Park; canvas-and-leather-gear manufacturer Frost River had moved in a year before. Nearby the Hansons opened OMC Smokehouse, a restaurant serving meats smoked on-site. Capitalizing on their shared dedication to craftsmanship, the three businesses organized the group Advancing Lincoln Park, and soon the neighborhood's commercial corridor became the Lincoln Park Craft District. Between 2014 and 2017 seventeen new businesses opened in the district, which now houses three breweries, two cideries, four leatherworks (including Duluth Pack, founded in the 1880s), a pottery, a creamery, several eateries, and the Duluth Folk School, which teaches classes on subjects from beekeeping to canoe restoration.

Duluth's craft movement is hardly contained within Lincoln Park. Most breweries are found downtown and in Canal Park, also home to Vikre Distillery, and restaurants throughout town serve locally sourced foods including pork from Carlton's Yker Acres farm and eggs from Wrenshall's Locally Laid Egg Company, operated by Duluthians.

Duluth's cultural expansion continued with the creation of a downtown arts district. As the city and the Fond du Lac Band argued in court, plans for a skywalk extension to connect the casino with the Sheraton Hotel were suspended. To facilitate the skywalk, the city had purchased three historic buildings, two of which housed the NorShor Theatre. The city now had to justify its purchase.

Ness pushed for the NorShor's renovation. The $30 million cost was partially offset with historic tax credits facilitated by partnering with Sherman Associates, the Sheraton's owner. While the project was underway in 2015, the city council passed a resolution designating a new Historic Arts and Theater District along Superior Street between Lake Avenue and Ninth Avenue East. As a "haven for the performing, visual and culinary arts," the HART District includes the NorShor, Teatro Zuccone, Zinema movie house, several eateries, three craft breweries, a coffee roaster, and the Fitger's complex.

An Unexpected Departure

In October 2014, with approval ratings approaching 90 percent, Ness announced he would not seek reelection. His successor, Democrat Emily Larson, proved equally popular, taking home 72 percent of the 2015 vote. The first woman elected the Zenith City's mayor, Larson is also the first nonnative Duluthian to hold the office since 1959. The St. Paulite came to Duluth for her education, earning degrees from both the College of St. Scholastica and UMD before becoming a city councilor in 2011. One of the signatures of Larson's tenure as mayor has been her administration's efforts to reduce the city's greenhouse gas emissions by 80 percent by 2050. Another has been its commitment to improving relations with the Native community.

As Larson replaced Ness, Wally Dupius took Diver's seat as the Fond du Lac Band's chair. The two new administrations negotiated a deal: the band agreed to pay Duluth $150,000 annually for public utilities, and the city dropped its pending litigation. The band's ultimate victory is emblematic of its resurgence. Since 1870 Duluth's Native American population has been less than three percent, and until recently their presence in and contributions to Duluth have been largely overlooked. While the 2010 census showed 2,134 Native Americans living in Duluth, the most ever recorded, by 2017 that number had dropped to 1,630.

Yet the Native community has displayed a growing confidence, finding its voice on a variety of issues. Besides the casino, in downtown Duluth—on properties that were once part of the Buffalo Tract—the band operates the Thunderbird-Wren Halfway House for those over-coming substance abuse, the Center for American Indian Resources, and the American Indian Community Housing Organization, which opened an Indigenous food market in 2020. The Duluth Indigenous Commission has been providing city officials with a Native perspective since 2002, and in 2019 it renamed Lake Place Gichi-ode' Akiing, Ojibwe for "A Grand Heart Place." That August Indigenous artists began creating a mural in the park honoring Chief Buffalo.

But the settlement didn't fix Duluth's ongoing street maintenance issue. In 2017 Duluth voters supported a Larson administration initiative when they overwhelmingly passed a referendum to increase local sales tax by 0.5 percent, with proceeds dedicated to street repair. It is

The Arising by Carla Stetson (with Almut Heer) expresses the idea that it takes "the support of the whole community to create peace." It graces Lake Place, landscape architect Kent Worley's award-winning urban park disguising a highway tunnel through downtown Duluth. In 2019 Lake Place was renamed Gichi-ode' Akiing, Ojibwe for "A Grand Heart Place." *Zenith City Press*

expected to raise $7 million each year, more than double the current budget, but whether that will be enough remains to be seen. Built on a hill and subject to continuous freeze-and-thaw cycles, Duluth's streets require constant maintenance.

A Challenging Future

Street repair is one of many problems facing the Zenith City. Duluth still needs solutions to finance the operation and maintenance of its massive and ever-expanding park system. Public financing of Spirit Mountain, the Lake Superior Zoo, and the Great Lakes Aquarium remains unpopular; the city and public continue to wrestle with what the future of public golf will look like; and the 1980 Duluth Public Library requires over $30 million in mechanical upgrades. The Donald J. Trump administration's proposed budget cuts to the Great Lakes Restoration Initiative could dramatically curtail pollution abatement in the lower St. Louis River, and proposed sulfide-ore copper mining adjacent to the Boundary Waters Canoe Area Wilderness threatens the future of the entire St. Louis River estuary and, consequently, Lake Superior. Meanwhile, two 2018 studies found the lake's water contains microplastics.

Despite the city's renewed image, its population has remained relatively stagnant since 1985. While Duluth has found a new identity in its outdoors, culture, and craft movements—and summer tourism thrives— many of the jobs those industries create do not pay a living wage or provide health care or retirement benefits. The lack of sustainable manufacturing jobs has consequently created huge economic disparities among Duluthians. With its top third of wage earners doing very well and its bottom two-thirds struggling, Duluth's economy reflects the nation's. Its aging housing stock contains more rentals than homesteads, and it desperately lacks affordable housing—an issue the city is finally confronting, assembling an affordable housing task force in 2019. And while it displays an eagerness to please high-end real estate developers, Duluth cannot seem to shake its long-held reputation as an unfriendly place to do business, a sentiment reflected by recent city council debates over the city's Earned Sick and Safe Time Ordinance

Duluth's Architectural Heritage

Duluth's rich history is reflected in its architectural landmarks, which are essential to its cultural identity and the ongoing success of heritage tourism. Until the 1880s, most Duluth buildings were simple affairs, wood-frame structures no architects laid claim to, few faced in brick and all but one or two—including the Henry Hill store and boardinghouse along Canal Park Drive, built about 1870—are long gone.

As Duluth boomed in the 1880s, architect George Wirth's Richardsonian Romanesque Revival buildings—trimmed with local sandstone—popped up along Superior Street. Most were erected by Wirth's Duluth construction foreman, Oliver Traphagen, who in 1886 took over as the booming city's premier architect. For the next ten years Traphagen designed dozens of homes and buildings, most now gone. Examples that remain include city hall (1889), the police headquarters and jail (1890), and First Presbyterian Church (1891).

Many architects contributed to Duluth's historic landmarks, including Emmet Palmer and Lucien Hall, designers of the 1892 Duluth High School (also known as Old Central), whose iconic clock tower rivals the aerial bridge as a symbol of the city. Nearby the wealthy had built opulent Victorian mansions in Ashtabula Heights, but as the affluent moved away from downtown in the 1890s Duluth's architects embraced eclecticism, building houses reflecting Tudor, Shingle-Style, Romanesque, Colonial, Federalist, Tudor, and Arts and Crafts traditions.

During this period several nationally renowned architects left their mark on Duluth, including Daniel Burnham (the Alworth Building and the St. Louis County Courthouse) and Bertram Goodhue (the Kitchi Gammi Club, St. Paul's Episcopal Church, and two others). Construction slowed after 1920, and during the Depression Duluth built only a few art deco or modernist buildings, most notably downtown's Medical Arts Building (1932), which still stands.

Many buildings constructed before 1920 were lost to urban renewal and highway expansion. Duluth's preservation movement emerged during the eastern highway expansion debate and consequently saved many historic Superior Street buildings between Fifth and Ninth Avenues East. Since 1975 the Duluth Preservation Alliance has promoted the retention of historic landmarks and celebrated renovation efforts.

Since the late 1990s, however, Duluth's city council has often ignored the recommendations of its advisory Historic Preservation Commission (HPC). The Ness administration sold off many historic buildings owned by the city and even attempted to strip the HPC of its power to designate buildings as landmarks, a move that would have jeopardized state funding for the city. Citizen-led efforts only delayed the demolition of the St. Louis County Jail (1923) and St. Peter's Church (1926)—it took private investors to retain the buildings. Meanwhile efforts to renovate the jail and the National Guard Armory (1915) have repeatedly stalled over the years; consequently—and ironically—many view those buildings today as arguments against preservation.

Yet when preservation can help Duluth achieve its goals, the city embraces it. During its legal battle with the Fond du Lac Band, the city denied the band's request to tear down the Carter Hotel (1929), a contributing building to downtown Duluth's Commercial Historic District east of Lake Avenue. But once the dispute was resolved, the demolition was allowed to proceed. The Commercial Historic District itself was created as a result of a lawsuit against the city brought to save historic buildings threatened by a city-supported project. Duluth also used historic tax credits to renovate the city-owned NorShor Theatre, and funds supporting the St. Louis River Corridor Initiative to renovate Wade Stadium, the nation's last WPA–era brick ballpark.

But to justify the demolition of the blighted Kozy Apartments—designed in 1889 by Traphagen as the six opulent townhouses of Pastoret Terrace—the city has argued in part that, despite the opinion of state experts, a masterwork of its quintessential historic architect does not contribute to the district. Further, the city chose not to carry out even basic maintenance on a building it wanted to demolish, thus making it impossible for others to renovate.

Pastoret Terrace and at least four other contributing buildings in the district—which includes most of the Historic Arts and Theater District—

were slated to fall by the end of 2020. Ironically, Duluth's two official historic districts are on their way to becoming devoid of their historic buildings. Meanwhile, iconic Old Central—owned by the school board, which renders the building ineligible for state and federal historic tax credits—needs an estimated $48.5 million in renovations and repairs.

When Pastoret Terrace, aka "The Kozy," was first built in 1889 (top), it was the most sought-after address in Duluth; today (bottom) it has become a symbol of urban blight. *Zenith City Press*

and a five-cent fee retailers must charge for single-use plastic bags. With a lack of quality jobs and a school district run by a board whose past dysfunction still lingers in its reputation, Duluth hasn't exactly been driving new residents to its shores. But there are signs that may be changing. While the Census Bureau's 2018 estimate indicates the city had lost 182 citizens since 2010, state demographers estimated in November 2019 that 87,213 people live in Duluth, an increase of 1.33 percent over the last decade.

There is plenty of hard work ahead for Larson, reelected with 65 percent of the vote in 2019, and her successors. But despite her popularity and a general approval of her policies, Mayor Larson's administration—like that of her predecessor—is not without its critics. Many Duluthians don't appreciate the administration's lack of transparency—Duluthians were shocked in 2019 to find out that $10 million generated by the 0.5 percent tax increase for road repair would be spent on an expansion of the city's medical district, a detail left out of all discussion on the referendum. Consequently the administration has been perceived by some as disrespectful to the general populace—particularly when it comes to parks, preservation, and development issues—as it aggressively pushes developer-friendly plans that have met with public opposition. It is a dynamic familiar to cities across the country.

Despite disagreements, the city's people continue to work together to find solutions. Until recently the city lobbied hard to remove what remains of the 1870 Lake Superior & Mississippi Railroad to make room for the extension of its Western Waterfront Trail as part of the St. Louis River Corridor Initiative. This would have doomed the modern LS&M, which offers excursion rides on the historic rail line. But after years of hard and often contentious work with the public, in autumn 2019 the city announced not only that it would retain the tracks but that the rail and trail routes would share the same corridor. Further, the trail would be renamed Waabizheshikana (Marten way, path, or road) a tribute to the Marten clan, an Ojibwe family who once lived in the area and created a system of footpaths and portages.

Entering its 150th year as a city, Duluth stands poised with promise. The 2019 legislative session was particularly kind to the Zenith City, with lawmakers passing Duluth's sales-tax increase and restoring over $700,000 in Local Government Aid from the Minnesota Department of Revenue the city lost in 2002. They also approved a $98.5 million appropriation bond for infrastructure improvements designed to complement the expansion of Duluth's health-care industry, which has grown steadily for decades. While St. Luke's Hospital, known today as St. Luke's Regional Health Care System, remains independent, St. Mary's Hospital, the Duluth Clinic, and Miller-Dwan Medical Center (formerly Miller Memorial Hospital) united by 2001; three years later they merged with the Benedictine Health System to become Essentia Health. In 2018 both Essentia and St. Luke's announced nearly $1 billion in major expansions, which will secure Duluth's future as the region's major medical center. Duluth has also quietly emerged as a center for higher education. Together, two-year Lake Superior College, the College of St. Scholastica,

The structure seen lying at the very northeastern corner of Lake Superior washed up adjacent to the Lakewalk in 2006. It is wooden cribbing that was submerged and filled with rocks ca. 1870 to act as the foundation for the infrastructure built by the Lake Superior & Mississippi Railroad to create Duluth's original waterfront. *Zenith City Press*

and UMD enroll more than twenty thousand students. Expansions of all three campuses over the past twenty years have created thousands of construction jobs; UMD alone has erected at least ten new buildings since 2000. In 2019, about one-third of Duluthians worked in health care, education, and social services—twice as many as those with manufacturing jobs.

The developments outlined in this chapter will eventually be viewed as successes, failures, or simply footnotes of their times. And as it has since 1856, Duluth will no doubt face unforeseen difficulties—but it will not face all of them alone. Duluth and Superior—the Twin Ports since 1910—began competing again in the 1950s as both struggled to survive the postwar industrial decline. A near-tragic 2018 explosion and fire at Superior's Husky oil refinery showed that the two communities still come together when it matters, as Duluth welcomed evacuating Superiorites and Mayor Larson and Jim Paine, her counterpart across the bay, have begun working together to make the refinery's operations safer.

Duluth and Superior are historically at their best when they work in tandem, particularly on issues that further connect them to the lake and river. Experts have predicted global warming will make the region a haven for wealthy climate-change refugees. Adjacent to ten percent of the planet's fresh water, the Twin Ports' relationship to Lake Superior and the St. Louis River—and to one another—has never been as important as it is today.

As Arthur W. Baum once suggested, Duluth is like a punch-drunk prizefighter who keeps getting up off the mat to face whatever confronts him. By continuing to embrace the lake and river, the city should find what it needs to survive and even thrive. And it would not hurt Duluthians to heed the wisdom of their predecessors: to accept Julius Barnes's challenge to believe in Duluth's "unlimited possibilities," to heed Sidney Luce's decree to "Do it for Duluth," and to strive to make Duluth Dr. Thomas Foster's "Zenith City of the Unsalted Seas."

Author's Note

In many ways I have been preparing to write this book since 2003, when first I stumbled across some vintage lithographic postcards of Duluth and thought it would be fun to create a full-color history book. Knowing very little about the city's history, I visited the Duluth Public Library's reference department, and there I met a wonderful team of librarians who in turn introduced me to Maryanne C. Norton, a volunteer researcher and a former director of the St. Louis County Historical Society. Maryanne's infectious passion for Duluth's history lit a fire under me that continues to burn, and I have since written and published more than a dozen books about the Zenith City's history. When I met Maryanne, I was just a writer without a topic; now they call me "historian." Maryanne died shortly before I began writing this book, but her lessons continue to guide me.

This book's goal is to tell Duluth's story as briefly as possible. Consequently its limited space forces the omission of many important events, issues, and actions that helped shape the city. Economy of words also restricts mentioning all of those who deserve credit—or in some cases blame—for their participation in the myriad civic projects and political and social developments that make up the city's history. Simply listing those whose hard work has made the Homegrown Music Festival a success would consume half a chapter. Similarly, this book's focus on Duluth's mayors serves to propel the narrative; the issues and events addressed herein have also been shaped by the efforts of countless aldermen, commissioners, city councilors, other elected or appointed public officials, city staff and administrators, and concerned Duluthians. To learn more about Duluth's rich history, please see "Further Reading" on the next page.

Besides Maryanne, many others helped with this book by providing research assistance and discussing Duluth's history with me, including Heidi Bakk-Hansen, Bob Berg, David Campbell, Pete Clure, Michael Cruikshank, Megan Dayton, Kyle Deming, John Fedo, Adam Fulton, Dan Hartman, Jim Heffernan, Richard Hudelson, Phil Jents, Dennis Lamkin, Emily Larson, Tim Lee, Konnie LeMay, Jeff Lemke, Paul Lundgren, Patricia Maus, Larry Millett, Don Ness, Scott Pearson, John Schwetman, Joel Sipress, Rabbi David Stenberg, Bruce White, and current and former librarians in the Duluth Public Library's Reference Department, including Kris Aho, Mike Grossman, Julie Kapke, Jess Korpi, Stacy LaVres, Julie Levang, Maureen Maloney, David Ouse, and Ellen Pioro. Others helped provide the images found in this book, including Pete Clure, the Duluth Public Library, John Fedo, Laura Jacobs and the Lake Superior Maritime Collection, the Library of Congress, the Minnesota Historical Society, Neal Ronquist of the *Duluth News Tribune,* and Shana Aue and Aimee Brown of the University of Minnesota Duluth's Kathryn A. Martin Library Archives and Special Collections.

And special thanks to Ann Regan and Shannon Pennefeather of the Minnesota Historical Society Press's editorial staff, along with freelance copyeditor Robyn Roslak, for their wonderful work wrestling with my words.

Further Reading

Readers looking for more Duluth and regional history may find these works of interest. A note for those seeking sources of direct quotations in the text: the reminiscences of early Duluthians appear in the books listed below by King, Van Brunt, and Woodbridge and Pardee; those of other Duluthians appear in Lydecker, et al.; and those within descriptions of civic projects from 1960 through 2017 can be found in *The Will and the Way* volumes 1 and 2 (edited by Gail Trowbridge and Jessica Tillman, respectively)—see notations at ends of citations. Other quotations from newspapers and periodicals can be found in the biography and subject clipping files in the reference department of the Duluth Public Library's main branch; many can also be found on internet archives. Please note that most of the stories in *The Will and the Way* books were written by those deeply involved in their subjects, often by those who spearheaded the efforts they describe, so while many contain insights not found in other sources, they also omit controversies and alternative perspectives about how events unfolded. Similarly, the books by Van Brunt and by Woodbridge and Pardee include recollections written down many years after the events took place, and most of the biographies found within Van Brunt were written by their subjects, who paid for their inclusion; consequently, the information these books contain should be checked against other sources. More information about Duluth's history can be found at zenithcity.com, including much of the content found in books listed below published by Zenith City Press.

Alanen, Arnold R. *Morgan Park: Duluth, U.S. Steel, and the Forging of a Company Town*. Minneapolis: University of Minnesota Press, 2007.

Baum, Arthur W. "Duluth." *Saturday Evening Post*, April 16, 1949. *(Full text available at zenithcity.com.)*

Beck, Bill, and C. Patrick Labadie. *Pride of the Inland Seas: An Illustrated History of the Port of Duluth-Superior*. Afton, MN: Afton Historical Society Press, 2004.

Cooley, Jerome. *Recollections of the Early Days in Duluth*. Duluth, MN: self-published by the author, 1922. *(Note: Many of Mr. Cooley's recollections are not accurate interpretations of history.)*

Dierckins, Tony. *Crossing the Canal: An Illustrated History of Duluth's Aerial Bridge*. Duluth, MN: Zenith City Press, 2008.

Dierckins, Tony, and Pete Clure. *Naturally Brewed, Naturally Better: The Historic Breweries of Duluth and Superior*. Duluth, MN: Zenith City Press, 2018.

Dierckins, Tony, and Nancy Nelson. *Duluth's Historic Parks: Their First 160 Years*. Duluth, MN: Zenith City Press, 2017.

Dierckins, Tony, and Maryanne C. Norton. *Lost Duluth: Landmarks, Industries, Buildings, Homes, and the Neighborhoods in Which They Stood*. Duluth, MN: Zenith City Press, 2012.

Fedo, Michael. *The Lynchings in Duluth*. St. Paul: Minnesota Historical Society Press, 2000.

Feichtinger, Gail, John DeSanto, and Gary Waller. *Will to Murder: The True Story of the Crimes and Trials Surrounding the Glensheen Killings*. 4th ed. Duluth, MN: Zenith City Press, 2009.

Flower, Frank A. *Eye of the Northwest: First Annual Report of the Statistician of Superior, Wisconsin*. Milwaukee, WI: King, Fowle, 1890.

Green, John C. "Why Is Lake Superior?" *The Minnesota Volunteer* 41, no. 239 (July–August 1978).

Hudelson, Richard, and Carl Ross. *By the Ore Docks: A Working People's History of Duluth*. Minneapolis: University of Minnesota Press, 2006.

Isaacs, Aaron. *Twin Ports by Trolley: The Streetcar Era in Duluth-Superior*. Minneapolis: University of Minnesota Press, 2014.

King, Frank A. *The Missabe Road: The Duluth, Missabe and Iron Range Railway*. San Marino, CA: Golden West Books, 1972. *(Includes the recollections of and excerpts of letter by William Banning.)*

Lamppa, Marvin G. *Minnesota's Iron Country: Rich Ore, Rich Lives*. Duluth, MN: Lake Superior Port Cities, 2004.

Lydecker, Ryck, Lawrence J. Sommer, and Arthur J. Larsen, eds. *Duluth, Sketches of the Past: A Bicentennial Collection*. Duluth, MN: American Revolution Bicentennial Committee, 1976. *(Includes the recollections of George D. Johnson,*

Harold Starin, and others that also appear in Van Brunt and Woodbridge and Pardee.)

MacDonald, Dora Mary. *This Is Duluth*. Duluth, MN: self-published by the author and printed by Duluth Central High School students, 1950.

Onigamiinsing Dibaajimowinan (Duluth Stories). Website created by the Fond du Lac Band of Lake Superior Chippewa, 2018. http://www.duluthstories.net.

Ouse, David. *Forgotten Duluthians*. Duluth, MN: X-presso Books, 2010.

Sargent, George B. *Lecture on the West*. Davenport, IA: Luse, Lane and Co., 1858.

Tillman, Jessica, ed. *The Will and the Way*. Vol. 2. Duluth, MN: published by Donn Larson, 2018.

Treuer, Anton. *Ojibwe in Minnesota*. St. Paul, MN: Minnesota Historical Society Press, 2010.

Trowbridge, Gail, ed. *The Will and the Way*. Vol. 1. Duluth, MN: published by Donn Larson and Manly Goldfine, 2004. *(Includes quotations attributed to John Fedo, Jerry Kimball, and Donn Larson.)*

Trowbridge, John Townsend. "A Week in Duluth." *Atlantic Monthly*, May 1870. *(Full text available at zenithcity.com.)*

Van Brunt, Walter. *Duluth and St. Louis County, Minnesota: Their Story and People*. 3 vols. New York: American Historical Society, 1921. *(Includes recollections from James Bardon, Leonidas Merritt, Robert Mitchell, and others, many of which also appear in Woodbridge and Pardee.)*

Warren, William W. *History of the Ojibwe People*. 2nd ed. St. Paul: Minnesota Historical Society Press, 2009.

Woodbridge, Dwight E., and John S. Pardee, eds. *History of Duluth and St. Louis County*. 2 vols. Chicago: C. F. Cooper, 1910. *(Includes recollections of John Carey, Edmund Ely, Sidney Luce, Robert McLean, Roger Munger, Julia Nettleton, and others, as well as characterizations of Vespasian Smith and Peter Dean.)*

Index